"Many Christians have memorized the words of Psalm 23, but do they truly understand their meaning? Heath Adamson reminds us of some of the familiar and surprising truths of this passage. After reading this book, you'll remember that even when you're in your valleys, God doesn't only provide comfort; he is alongside you with a perspective clearer than your own."

Mark Batterson, *New York Times* bestselling author of *The Circle Maker* and lead pastor of National Community Church

"Heath has the gift of bringing fresh insights to favorite passages. *Grace in the Valley* expands our vision of the shepherd who is with us and comforts us in all things."

Kara Powell, PhD, executive director of the Fuller Youth Institute and coauthor of *Growing Young*

"In my experience serving the poor and suffering and meeting needs around the world, I have experienced firsthand how hopelessness can imprison someone. You don't need to travel very far, however, to encounter someone whose experience doesn't line up with what they know to be true about God. He is good. He is loving. He is compassionate and near. Whether we identify with the poor and suffering who don't know where to turn or with someone in the suburbs who sits in quiet desperation, God is trustworthy even if our situation seems to give us a reason not to believe so. Heath Adamson is a trusted global voice, a close friend, and an emerging author I highly recommend. He has walked the valley of the shadow of death along with the rest of us. Let him summon you to dare to believe in God's goodness regardless of your experience."

Hal Donaldson, president of Convoy of Hope

"If we are the patients and verses of Scripture our medicine, then Psalm 23 is spiritual penicillin, a cure-all for the postmodern predicament. In *Grace in the Valley*, Heath Adamson wrestles through one of the Bible's most beloved and important passages, uncovering lost wisdom we all need to rediscover. In a time of increasing chaos, uncertainty, and fear, Adamson reminds us that God has a green pasture for us all, even in the midst of life's greatest battles."

Rev. Samuel Rodriguez, president of the National
Hispanic Christian Leadership Conference

"Anyone can see beauty from the mountaintop. Heath dares us to see beauty in the valley of shadows, where so many of us live so often. A must-read for all in suffering. Seeing light in darkness is our native birthright, and Heath eloquently points the way to that light. May we all have eyes to see beauty and light in valleys of our lives."

Ted Dekker, *New York Times* bestselling author

"Heath's fresh perspective on an old passage is a powerful look at painful places. His thoughtful rendering of Psalm 23 is a tangible reminder of hope. For anyone walking through a dark time, this book will remind you to take heart—because shadows serve to remind us that there's something beyond what we see. And that every place in our journey is filled with grace."

Rob Hoskins, president of OneHope Inc.

GRACE
in the
VALLEY

Awakening to God's Presence
When He Feels Far Away

HEATH ADAMSON

BakerBooks
a division of Baker Publishing Group
Grand Rapids, Michigan

Published by Baker Books
a division of Baker Publishing Group
PO Box 6287, Grand Rapids, MI 49516-6287
www.bakerbooks.com

Printed in the United States of America

Library of Congress Cataloging-in-Publication Data
Names: Adamson, Heath, 1977– author.
Title: Grace in the valley : awakening to God's presence when he feels far away / Heath Adamson.
Description: Grand Rapids, MI : Baker Books, [2018]
Identifiers: LCCN 2018014415 | ISBN 9780801093715 (pbk.)
Subjects: LCSH: Bible. Psalms, XXIII—Criticism, interpretation, etc. | Hidden God.
Classification: LCC BS1450 23d .A33 2018 | DDC 223/.20—dc23
LC record available at https://lccn.loc.gov/2018014415

In keeping with biblical principles of creation stewardship, Baker Publishing Group advocates the responsible use of our natural resources. As a member of the Green Press Initiative, our company uses recycled paper when possible. The text paper of this book is composed in part of post-consumer waste.

19 20 21 22 23 24 25   8 7 6 5 4 3 2

Thank you, Father,
for "Even the darkness is not dark to you"
(Ps. 139:12).

To Ali:
this book is dedicated to you. I am not worthy
to live and dream with you. I love you more.

To Leighton and Dallon:
may our spiritual ceiling become your floor.

To Ted:
thank you for showing us the heart of Jesus.

To Dan and Kathy at Creative Trust:
thank you for daring to listen.

To Brian and the team at Baker Publishing:
this work is a collaborative one. I honor you for working
so hard to cause someone else's faith walk to be known.

And finally:
I am grateful for the many people along the way who have
shaped the content of this book over the past twenty-three
years. I am a product of every interaction. Thank you.

Contents

Introduction

But I Still Love You

Her valley began in second grade.

A tumultuous childhood, abuse, unpredictable parents, and deep darkness made it difficult for the young girl to sit still in the classroom. She was royalty and didn't know it. She was loved but no one treated her as such. All she knew, at such a young age, was that life was hard and God was far away.

Her teacher, frustrated beyond belief with the young girl's antics and misbehavior, had finally reached her limit, and she turned to the young girl's peers as a last attempt for a solution. A vicious solution. There is no way the teacher knew how deep the darkness would be. "I want everyone to come up to the chalkboard, one by one, and write down everything you think about her," the teacher thundered.

There is no way any of the students could comprehend, at such a young age, how much of an impact their actions would have. And so it began. One by one the students walked up to the chalkboard and wrote down how they felt about the young girl. Their words were far from kind.

"Nobody likes you."

"You're stupid."

"Dumby."

"Just go home!"

One word after another, written with chalk on the slate board but carved in stone on the young girl's heart, became much more than a rant or an opinion. The words were prophetic. If only someone was there to show her, at such a vulnerable time and in such a fragile state, that even there, in the midst of that pain, was love. It would take her years to remember that, in her darkest valley, a bloom had appeared.

That second-grade girl matured too fast and aged too quickly. By her early twenties, she had experienced decades of pain in a few years. After a few failed marriages, a life of prostitution, children turned over to the state, and a body racked by substance abuse, she finally tried to take her own life. She made promises and never kept them. She regretted the day her children were taken away. Those around her assumed she built walls to keep them out. She would tell you she built walls to see who loved her enough to climb over them. She was ashamed to look her parents in the eye. She was ashamed to look in the mirror.

Ending it once and for all was the only way. But she was such a failure, she assumed, she couldn't even take her own life correctly. After her failed attempt at suicide, her parents were strongly cautioned to seek professional psychiatric help. In a last-ditch attempt to save their daughter's life, they made the appointment. Maybe a heavy regimen of medication could save her? She walked into the doctor's office alone as her parents waited in the lobby.

That's when her valley began to bloom.

The doctor was aware of her past. He knew she had lost everything. He could see in her eyes the emptiness she longed to forget. "Tell me about your childhood, especially those elementary years," he said. She began to recount the typical things like play at recess, crushes on boys, the games young girls play when they feel threatened, and the abuse. The abuse? That's when the doctor probed further, as this was new to him.

She recounted in detail how her childhood had been stolen from her. It culminated that day in second grade when her peers prophesied on that chalkboard not what they thought but who she believed herself to be. She sat in his office, weeping, as the doctor walked her through a process known as reflection. She could still see the smirks on the faces of her classmates as they pointed, laughed, and jeered. She sat there, crying, hoping someone would rescue her. There was no one to be found. It was the most painful moment of her life.

Unjust. Unfair. Evil.

She couldn't take the embarrassment any longer. Crying in front of someone was not her style, and she certainly didn't want to do so with someone who was paid to care about her. She got up from the chair, shut down the counseling session, and moved toward the door.

"I am not finished yet. Come back and sit down."

His voice shocked her. The audacity of the doctor—to so boldly assume he had the right to speak to her that way.

"I mean it. I have something to say."

For some reason, she didn't run away like she usually did. Not this time. She turned around, sat down in the chair, wiped her tears and nose, and looked at him.

"You forgot the most important part of that day in the classroom. Remember that little boy who walked up to the board and wrote these words: 'I still love you'? I was that boy. I remember you, and for years I wondered what happened to you."

Right then and there, it clicked in her heart as she realized that in the darkest moment of her life she had been loved. As a child, had she ignored the words the boy wrote or turned away just before he began writing? Maybe she had seen the words clearly but relegated them to mere sarcasm? She didn't remember. Pain masquerades as our friend when being vulnerable takes too much courage. Whether she dismissed it, ignored it, or simply did not see love bloom in front of her, she lived for years listening to all of those voices—all but one. The most important one.

Her valley, though saturated in shadows and death, was in bloom. Love drew near and invited her to dare to believe her value. And for all those years, she didn't realize how worth it she truly was.

Maybe you don't realize how much you are worth either.

Embracing the display of love from that young boy, though it wouldn't erase what the others said, would certainly have eclipsed it. That's what love does. It summons us to the deep place of being vulnerable where what we see is not all there is.

The Mystery

We can wonder if God comes through for everyone but us. We can feel like he is just no longer interested in hearing our cry for clarity and hope. We are convinced we just messed up too many times. We pretend something no longer bothers us. It feels right to think God is mad at us. It feels right to think he gives up on us. It feels right to think we were just created for the mess we are in, that we deserve it, and that it's simply our lot in life.

You can't always believe everything you feel.

That young girl felt worthless in second grade because of what others thought, said, and did to her. Does that not mean she could have felt loved, valued, and like the royalty she was, had she believed what that boy wrote?

You may relate to a cancer diagnosis, a childhood riddled with abuse, a marriage laden with disappointment, depression, an opioid addiction, or a life racked with financial hardship or loneliness. You may not sleep well at night because of your worries. You may not even feel like there is a reason to smile or laugh anymore. You may have all life has to offer and still feel there's something missing. It's mysterious when everyone else's prayers seem to be answered but not yours. It's mysterious when things work out for them but never for you.

Why mysterious?

We know God spoke the stars into existence and intervening in our situation is easy for him. We know God can and wonder why he doesn't. Or we choose not to wonder and pretend it's all okay. Why doesn't he come to us in our deep need? Why didn't he prevent the painful mystery from happening to begin with? We are stuck with the all-too-familiar conclusion that it must simply be that God either isn't interested, doesn't care, is not as good as he says he is, or doesn't find us worthy enough to step in and prevent the pain.

What if preventing something isn't the primary purpose of love?

Like that little girl, we may give up just before the eyes of our heart see the display of God's love in front of us. We may even feel like the love of God we see is too good to be true. When the valley of the shadow of death blooms, it doesn't mean our circumstances change or our problem goes away. It simply means we learn to see how loved we are. Solving the mystery is our goal. Answering the spiritual question is our journey. Eradicating the pain and hurt is our solution. Is there something better than these?

Scripture tells us that "the passion of love bursting into flame is more powerful than death, stronger than the grave" (Song 8:6 CEV). If love is stronger, why, then, doesn't death just go away? Why doesn't love stop the greatest of all enemies if it is stronger? Love demonstrates its strength not by preventing the weaker and painful things from happening. Love reveals its profound essence when, though it can win, it chooses to come alongside us and hold us. By not preventing the valley but revealing itself in it, love's great strength is revealed and the object of love's attention—you—have your breath taken away. The love of God doesn't need to prevent anything or perform a miracle to prove itself.

There is something even more miraculous than a miracle. It is embracing the reality that we are loved and deeply valued even in the valley.

The Pasture and the Valley

Love, in its deepest form, is often seen in the shadows.

Psalm 23 beckons us to discover how that love is graciously given in the most unlikely places. It invites us to a haven of intimacy with God when he may seem most distant. One of the most powerful and poetic passages in the entire Bible, from what we infer is David's writing, is the canvas on which I hope to reveal the contours and colors of this love before you:

> The LORD is my shepherd; I shall not want.
>> He makes me lie down in green pastures.
> He leads me beside still waters.
>> He restores my soul.
> He leads me in paths of righteousness
>> for his name's sake.
>
> Even though I walk through the valley of the shadow
>> of death,
>> I will fear no evil,
> for you are with me;
>> your rod and your staff,
> they comfort me.
>
> You prepare a table before me
>> in the presence of my enemies;
> you anoint my head with oil;
>> my cup overflows.
> Surely goodness and mercy shall follow me
>> all the days of my life,
> and I shall dwell in the house of the LORD
>> forever.

The twenty-third psalm is familiar to many of us. Those of the Judeo-Christian faith hear it frequently at funerals. Those still seeking words to wrap around their deep longing for spiritual truth, though they find less comfort in religion, still find it in these words. Much of the psalm is memorized, even if unintentionally, by people throughout the world. Fifty-seven Hebrew words, with a few more in current-day languages, take us all to that place where we ask why God would spread his banqueting table in the valley of the shadow of death and not the green pasture.

Why would David, the newly chosen king of a nation, refer to God as a shepherd rather than a mighty warrior or ruler? Why did David, though isolated and starving to death when this psalm originated, say he wanted nothing? If God could bring down Goliath, why didn't God bring down those who were trying to murder David? Why did God lead him into the valley of the shadow of death when God could easily take a detour to a greener pasture? In all of our differences in culture, gender, religion, and background, we are all united through the pain and deep longing we experience when our circumstances do not align with our hope in God's character. We experience the hard times, though often not written in chalk, and wonder why God allowed them to occur. We long for the green pasture when we walk through the valley of the shadow of death.

But remember, Scripture says it's only a shadow.

Do you know that, regardless of what people have said to you or what you've done, God writes on your chalkboard, "I still love you"?

ONE

Learning to See

The LORD is my shepherd.

I
t is easy, comfortable, and merely human to reduce life to what we see, but your story and my story are being written by the Unseen One.

We squint and stare to read the fine print. Our challenge is not that God writes in computer coding or with complex algorithms. That would only spur us on to crack his code and translate his message. No, he writes with something offensive to our minds and concealed to our understanding.

Mystery.

Chances are, you have been in a Starbucks at least once in your life. If you are part of the rare group who hasn't, I applaud your discipline to either avoid coffee or frequent the local barista. Regardless, the majority of us are aware of the unique language Starbucks uses. I remember when I first learned not to say the word *medium* and rather to use the word *grande*. The Starbucks barista did not scold me, scorn me, throw me out of the establishment, or acquiesce to my language. No, the barista did something unusual. My order was simply repeated back to me using their lingo. If I ordered a "medium bold coffee with cream," as I paid, I was informed my "grande dark roast with room" was on the way.

Walk into a Dunkin' Donuts and ask for a grande and they will give you a medium. Order a medium at Starbucks and they will give you a grande. The language doesn't change what you're getting. The language changes your understanding of it.

When we ask God for a miracle in our heart, marriage, home, school, generation, way of thinking, or fill-in-the-blank, he hears us clearly and coherently. When you ask for a *miracle*, God gives it to you, but most often it comes packaged as a *mystery*.

To be clear, Scripture reminds us that our adversary is the author of confusion. God writes not with confusion but mystery. Mysteries are not intended to confuse. They are an invitation to look closely, maybe not at something new but rather something that has been there all along and merely overlooked. We must learn to embrace the mystery without wavering in our confidence in God's character.

Most often, mysteries reveal our heart. Jesus spoke in mystery for this reason (Matt. 13:11). He said so himself. The educated and intellectual elite wrestled with the mental maze the teachings of Jesus provided, yet the little children flocked at his feet as if they felt comfortable with the conversation Jesus offered. Why were children comfortable with him and the educated offended? Perhaps because children see beyond. Mystery is beautiful to them.

But mystery is just plain scary to us. Our educated and experienced minds churn to force all of life's experiences into a mental file. We don't want the clutter; indeed, we cannot even tolerate it most of the time. Our schemas file both the good and bad in a way our hearts can survive. Annoyed by the dysfunction of mystery, we go around them to start again tomorrow. Our prayer lives can evolve into a passive-aggressive pattern as we seek control by knowing, predicting, and pretending to understand.

What do you do when your circumstances do not line up with the goodness of the One you read about in Scripture?

What do you do when what you see does not agree with what your heart knows to be true about God?

Some of us blame God; some ignore him; some try to be him. Inquire of anyone who has implemented these strategies and been successful—and you will find none. We must become good at unlearning what we think we know and less skilled at knowing (1 Cor. 8:2). Mystery is one of the primary means God uses to invite us into a deeper understanding of his love.

Of the 125 unique teaching incidents of Jesus recorded in the Gospels, thirteen begin with statements and the rest start with questions. The primary methods Jesus employed in his teaching can be reduced to asking questions and telling stories (parables). God clothed truth and love and came to walk among us. His goal was not merely to teach us what to believe; he came to teach us how to believe. A follower of Jesus does not just believe what Jesus believes but how Jesus believes. As someone once said, "We do not memorize Jesus; we become like him."

One of the primary ways we become like him is to enter into one of his parables and live in the mystery where our circumstance, or our understanding of it, exposes where our heart truly is. If mystery was valuable to Jesus when he reintroduced

God to the world, it is valuable to us today. In our valleys, Jesus summons us to peer into the mystery and there discover the miracle.

Learning How to See from the Blind Men

This kind of seeing does not come to us easily. Come with me to that moment recorded in Matthew 20 when God was about to walk past the blind beggar.

> And as they went out of Jericho, a great crowd followed him. And behold, there were two blind men sitting by the roadside, and when they heard that Jesus was passing by, they cried out, "Lord, have mercy on us, Son of David!" The crowd rebuked them, telling them to be silent, but they cried out all the more, "Lord, have mercy on us, Son of David!" And stopping, Jesus called them and said, "What do you want me to do for you?" They said to him, "Lord, let our eyes be opened." And Jesus in pity touched their eyes, and immediately they recovered their sight and followed him. (vv. 29–34)

Jericho, the "moon city" or "city of palms," is the place that comes to mind when we think of Joshua.

Remember?

It's the place where the walls supernaturally fell down (Josh. 6). Jericho is approximately six miles north of the Dead Sea. In the middle of the desert, it was an oasis. An underground spring caused it to bloom regardless of the surrounding environment—a real-life "valley of the shadow of death" blooming. Known as a fertile place, it was only a matter of time before Jericho became a stop for travelers on the way from the highlands of Judah to the Trans Jordan. Built on top of a mound and fortified with a double wall, Jericho was basically unconquerable.

Moses warned the Israelites, with the Promised Land near, of cities "great and fortified up to heaven" (Deut. 9:1). The sudden invasion and destruction of the city would have caught the attention of nearby cities, and rumors of the great God Jehovah would spread far and wide. Regardless of one's religious beliefs, Jericho became synonymous with the fact that a God you don't see can supernaturally intervene in the circumstances you do see.

Hundreds of years later, God would clothe himself with skin and personally walk beside the ruins. In the valley of Jericho (Deut. 34:3), a city of broken walls was now a city filled with broken people. Among them were two blind men, begging and helpless, in the very place where God had once sovereignly demonstrated his power.

Where was God now?

Why would God bring down walls but not open blind eyes?

Maybe the blind men laid their heads against a stone at night to find some relief for their sore necks. A stone God himself had brought down, which used to comprise the wall.

I can just imagine a father and mother walking down the road with their two daughters. One of the little girls asks, "Daddy, why is that big pile of bricks over there? Where did they come from?"

"Well, sweetie. Let me tell you a story. You see, a long time ago, the very ground you stand on was traveled by many. People came from all over to Jericho. I know it doesn't seem like much now. But there was a day when this was one of the great cities. That pile of stones you see over there is evidence there used to be a very tall and very thick wall protecting this city. But then the God who is highly exalted, the One you currently do not see, caused those walls to fall down in order to give his people the victory."

"Daddy, if God is so powerful and can knock walls down, why doesn't he heal those blind beggars over there?"

If the father is like many of us, in a circumstance that seems to contradict God's goodness, we may respond like I imagine him doing: "Maybe it's a fairy tale, honey. God didn't knock those walls down. If it really was God, then surely he would see the condition of those blind men and help them. The fact that they sit there, blind, is evidence enough for me that God isn't as good as people think. Maybe he isn't even there at all."

And just then, with the dust kicking up from his sandals, Jesus of Nazareth would've walked by that family as the blind men cried out, "Son of David, have mercy on us!" What a story they would have to tell of a life transformed by mercy!

How can I imagine someone accusing God by comparing his past goodness to his present inaction? Because I've done so myself. I've seen God come through just in time only to fret and worry the next time a need arose. I've believed God can perform miracles only to think he wouldn't do so for me when I was sick. I've encouraged others to pray and shared stories of answered prayers only to feel as if my prayers weren't enough when I faced a trial the next day. I know what it's like to look at the evidence, that great big pile of stones that comprised the wall God knocked down, and use the "blind beggars by the Jericho road" in my life to doubt his goodness.

I remember the first blind beggar I came in contact with.

I was walking down the streets of the beautiful and historic city of Antigua, Guatemala. Known for some of the world's greatest coffee, Antigua is a hot spot for tourists. I was there with a group doing some humanitarian and missional work. I walked down the street with a friend and was completely caught off guard by a melody I heard. I just knew that I knew that music, even if the words were in a language I did not understand. I stopped on the cobblestone sidewalk and turned to see a man sitting by the curb singing the old Christian hymn "Amazing Grace." As I looked, my astonishment at hearing a familiar tune in that old village was soon overrun by my astonishment at the man's condition. He had no legs or arms, and he was blind.

His outer appearance gave clues that bathing was something he didn't or couldn't do. I mean no disrespect, but he was just filthy. His hair was matted. He sat on the curb surrounded by natives and wealthy tourists and begged for money. Instantly moved, I reached into my pocket to take out some money and began walking toward him. I felt my friend firmly grab my arm and stop me.

"Just wait a second. I need to see if he is really in need."

I was appalled. *Really in need?* The man had no legs, no arms, and by this time we could see his eyes were as white as wool. It didn't take a PhD to figure out he was in need. It didn't even take a diploma from a kindergarten graduation class to see this man had no hope unless someone gave to him.

That's when my friend explained to me something I didn't understand. He said many of the beggars with disabilities in the country were victims of human trafficking. In bazaars where tourists shopped for souvenirs or humanitarian workers purchased supplies, the beggars were strategically placed. Those physically or mentally disabled, little children, and the elderly were often trafficked to meet a quota by begging. The dilemma is this: if you don't give to them and they don't meet their quota, their bosses beat them and abuse them for not bringing back enough money. If you do give to them and they exceed their quota, then the quota is raised and you make it more difficult for the beggar in the long run. My friend, who lived near Antigua, needed to find out if this beggar was legitimately begging and able to keep the money or if he was a victim of human trafficking. The answer to this would determine our response in how to meet the need.

The blind beggar continued singing in Spanish and came to the line in the hymn that goes like this: *I once was lost but now am found, was blind but now I see.* Some of these victims of human trafficking used religion as a cloak for their activity. You may think giving financially to a beggar regardless of their legitimacy or sincerity is good. But remember, perpetuating human trafficking is different than giving to the poor. The world we live in is very complex. And sometimes we complicate what should just be simple. Having compassion and meeting a need requires both wisdom and simplicity. We see this in the life of Christ. After all, he asked a crippled beggar if he truly wanted to be healed. This seems insincere to our western minds, but Jesus did nothing that wasn't motivated by and demonstrated through love. He used the question to reveal the beggar's heart. My friend did something similar by walking up to the beggar, kneeling down, and whispering in his ear, "My friend, if God's grace is so amazing, then why do you sit here beside the road, blind, singing of a God who can heal your blindness?"

I'll never forget the look on his face when the blind beggar abruptly stopped singing and responded. I was told he said in response, "My good friend, if you don't think God's grace is amazing, then you are more blind than I am." These words brought with them a peace and clarity only truly knowing God can bring. My friend started crying, and so did I. We realized that meeting the man's legitimate need could be as simple as placing some money underneath his hip and letting him know the amount so no one would cheat him. That blind man in Antigua taught me how to see that day. Just like the blind men in the valley of Jericho.

I want you to notice something in the story we see in Matthew's Gospel. The blind men cried out not fully sure that Jesus was there. After all, they were blind. How did they really know he was there? But just because we can't see him doesn't mean he isn't near. They cried out, not for healing or money but for mercy. At that time, the crowd asked them to be quiet. We can infer from the text they told the men to shut up. So the beggars cried out even louder. The word we translate "cry out" means to scream and shriek. They were far from dignified.

They were desperate.

There is a place of vulnerability we must arrive at in our need. Some of us become ashamed of what people think. We sit in quiet desperation, assuming being alone is better than being authentic. Remaining silent when you are by the road in life, begging, can prevent you from encountering the very One who is near you. What I know from Matthew 20 is this: if the blind men had remained silent, Jesus very well could have walked out of that city and they would have spent the rest of their lives begging and blind. They couldn't see those who ridiculed them. They were blind to those who snickered and sneered. They obviously didn't allow their reputation or embarrassment or what others thought keep them from asking God for mercy. When we get to the place where we see no one else around but God, our priorities change.

Jesus continued to walk. A detailed study of the Gospels reveals Jesus is about to wrap up his public ministry and enter into Jerusalem for what will soon become the passion week. Why didn't Jesus stop the first time they cried out? Did he hear them and ignore them? Was it so noisy that Jesus couldn't hear? We don't know. What we do know is that they cried out again. Sometimes we cry out to God once and, when we don't think we get his attention, we make excuses and stop. Sometimes we use God's sovereignty as an excuse to quit. Sometimes we build a theology around why God didn't respond the first time we cried out. What I get when I read the story in Matthew 20 is that it's okay to cry out more than once. Jesus didn't correct them for crying out a second time.

He stopped.

He looked. He asked, "What do you want me to do for you?"

Their response? They wanted to see. In the Greek New Testament, the blind men asked Jesus to heal their *ophthalmoi* (meaning biological eyes). Jesus touched their *ommata*, a word Plato used poetically to describe the eyes of the soul. Jesus touched their *ommata* first, and then their *ophthalmoi* worked properly. The eyes of their soul were opened. I submit to you that there, in the valley of Jericho, a barren place except for one little area where an underground spring irrigated the ground, the blind men saw a valley of the shadow of death in full bloom. God prepared a table for them in the presence of their blindness, poverty, and brokenness.

What caught God's attention in the ancient city of Jericho in Joshua 6 and Matthew 20 was not the condition of his children but their passion. Whether it's walking around the wall seven times in worship and watching it fall or crying out to God when he is about to pass by, there are times when our love for God in the valley causes us to cry out and worship him regardless of what we see and feel.

When our loved one is sick, we thank God for them and pray. When we can't sleep, we go to Scripture and trust God when we think we can't. When prayer is too hard, we lay down in silence knowing he's not threatened by it. If a friend asks how we are doing, we avoid the trite answer and vulnerably express to them what's going on. We go to someone who loves us and ask them to pray for us. We rummage through our pantry or cabinets and find something to celebrate communion with. In all these things and more, we reach beyond how we feel and dare to embrace his love for us.

What I know is that when I lay beside the road, rather than blame God for why I cannot see, I will cry out to him time and time again, for I know he is near. When we peer deeply through the pain, we begin to see God's goodness and also see the mystery we face as a divine invitation to walk down the path, often a lonely one, toward the valley of the shadow of death.

There, in the valley, surrounded by the enemy and death, we experience the miracle of seeing. There is something else written on the chalkboard of our soul we have forgotten: our name inscribed with the divine hand reserving a seat for us at God's table. Often, God invites us into moments we would choose to avoid to catch a glimpse of the table only he can prepare. A table we, as children of the King, can feast at as sons and daughters.

See?

God's grace *is* amazing.

The scroll of the ancient prophet Isaiah reminds us that God "hides himself" (Isa. 45:15).

Proverbs 25:2 invites royalty, like you and me, to seek out what he hides.

It is not happenstance the Hebrew Sabbath begins at sunset, when darkness begins to lurk and our vision grows dim. Psalm 104:20 says "He sends the night and darkness" (TLB). We remember him in the twilight, when what we see becomes difficult to make out. For in this we truly see.

There are times when God, often described in Scripture as our Father, takes us by the hand and lures us to the barren place so we can have front row seats as he makes it bloom.

The Barren Place Can Bloom

More than four thousand miles wide, the Sahel lies just below the Sahara Desert. May through August brings twelve months' worth of rainfall. As you can imagine, eight months without rain profoundly affects life. The desert floor cracks. Eyes burn. Dust blows everywhere. Mirages on the horizon become commonplace. Humans and animals alike crave a drop of water, a bite of food. One wonders how long this area can sustain life.

Del Tarr, a missionary and advocate for the underserved, lived on the border of the Sahara for over twenty years and observed this place firsthand. He knew the lonely roads well and recalled how a brief rainy season meant that farmers grew, harvested, and rationed their year's worth of food, such as sorghum and milo, in a few short months.

The months of October and November were filled with celebration. Harvest filled the granaries with food. In the villages, each adult and child enjoyed a luxurious two meals a day. Using ancient stones to grind the grain into flour, the villagers lived off what Del described as "yesterday's cream of wheat." The mush, while hot, is rolled into little balls and sometimes dipped in sauce. With full stomachs, they sleep.

In December, grain begins to run low and families skip breakfast to conserve food. In January, one meal per day is their sustenance.

In February, the one meal enjoyed by everyone grows smaller. Children become sick in March as their immune systems are weakened from malnourishment. One-half of a meal a day just isn't enough.

Here is how Del Tarr graphically described the plight of these people:

April is the month that haunts my memory. You hear the babies crying in the twilight. They pass most days with only an evening cup of gruel.

Then, inevitably, it happens. One day a six- or seven-year-old boy comes running to his father, bursting with excitement. "Daddy! Daddy! We've got grain!" he shouts.

The father calms him down and replies, "Son, you know we haven't had grain for weeks."

"Yes, we have!" the boy insists. "Out in the hut where we keep the goats I found a leather sack hanging up on the wall. When I put my hand inside the sack I felt the grain. There's grain in the sack! Give it to Mommy so she can make flour, and tonight our tummies can sleep!"

The father stands motionless.

"Son, we can't do that," he gently explains. "The seeds in that sack are next year's seed grain. Those seeds are the only thing between us and starvation. We're keeping the grain until the rains come again. Then we'll plant it."

The rains finally arrive in May, and when they do the young boy watches his father take the sack from the wall and do the most unreasonable thing imaginable. Instead of feeding his desperately weakened family, he walks to the field and, with tears streaming down his face, he takes the precious seed and scatters it in the soil. Why? Because he believes in the harvest.[1]

The father took the child by the hand and traversed the space that served only as a reminder that things all around were depleting, barren, and even dead. The father saw what the child could not see. The father saw the days to come. The father modeled the importance of taking what is most precious to us and becoming vulnerable even in the most desolate of places.

When we walk the path of mystery we are tempted to hoard what we have left. In relationships, we are tempted to close off a piece of our heart when we are wounded. In finance, we are tempted to say goodbye to generosity when we fear a financial collapse. In hope, we refuse to believe again, for we cannot afford to be let down another time. In second grade, we believe the lies written on the chalkboard.

One of my favorite names used in Scripture for Jesus is "a root out of dry ground" (Isa. 53:2 NKJV). It's interesting to me that when planting his Son in the world, God chose an environment and landscape similar to the Sahel: a place where life isn't supposed to grow. The Savior came to love all of us, even when we feel as if we are in the classroom all alone, experiencing deep pain like the little girl. God causes things to grow when they aren't supposed to. Why? Because to him, things aren't necessarily dead; they're merely dormant. This is what Moses experienced in another desert.

A World Aflame with the Divine

Most of us know the story.

At the age of forty, Moses murdered an Egyptian, and someone discovered his crime. In order to save his own life, he fled Egypt and vanished into the Sinai Peninsula. For forty years, he tended sheep under the hot African sun. He married and began a family. The past he had tried to bury in the sand became a fading memory.

At the age of eighty, on a day like all other days, Moses watched the sun come up over the Horeb mountains. The shadow from Mt. Horeb brought relief from the heat as the desert winds churned up dust like the dry soil of the African Sahel. On that day, as Moses walked past a bush, he noticed something that forever altered his understanding of God.

> Now Moses was keeping the flock of his father-in-law, Jethro, the priest of Midian, and he led his flock to the west side of the wilderness and came to Horeb, the mountain of God. And the angel of the LORD appeared to him in a flame of fire out of the midst of a bush. He looked, and behold, the bush was burning, yet it was not consumed. And Moses said, "I will turn aside to see this great sight, why the bush is not burned." When the LORD saw that he turned aside to see, God called to him out of the bush, "Moses, Moses!" And he said, "Here I am." Then he said, "Do not come near; take your sandals off your feet, for the place on which you are standing is holy ground." (Exod. 3:1–5)

Moses "turned aside to see" and *then* God spoke. There are some aspects of the spiritual life that God waits to share with us until we turn aside. Even when our situation is void and barren, we must remember we are called to his voice. Turning aside can be a time of prayer and reflection or journaling. We turn aside when we read Scripture. Turning aside can be much more than a spiritual discipline. It is a posture of heart that dares to believe God is near even when we don't feel so.

Moses saw the mystery—a bush on fire but not consumed. The Hebrew word for "saw" is *ra'ah*, which can mean "to see with the eyes of the soul." Rabbis teach the bush had been on fire for quite some time, and Moses slowed down long enough to notice. To notice what? A world aflame with divine and spiritual realities. It makes you wonder how many other people walked past the bush unaware that God was there . . . waiting . . . with something to say.

It was in the desolate place near Mt. Horeb that Moses encountered who God truly was. Just because you experience something you don't understand does not mean God is absent. Maybe you need to know that even in your desperate or broken places, your world is aflame with the divine. When you turn aside to God, he will not turn you away.

It was in the dry place of the Sahel an earthly father saw beyond. Like him, God comes and takes us by the hand, for we do not walk alone. Though barren, the harvest field will produce again. God prepares a table for us in the valley. Maybe you need a reminder that the rainy season will come again, and those seeds of prayer and faith, hidden to the naked eye, will one day bloom.

In the Garden of Eden, God took a handful of dirt, breathed on it, and formed humanity. God spoke the world into existence, but he saved his very breath for us. God can breathe life into dead things.

Grace stands before you, like Jesus did the blind men, under the warm Jericho sun. Love stops in Person when you cry out to him. Love meets a spiritual need as the eyes of your soul are opened by God himself. You may have cried out before with your whole heart only to feel unheard. Your desperation is not in vain when it is directed toward God. When you cry out to him, God will stop for you too. There is a grace for your valley.

David lived through the spiritually dry season, felt the dust in his face, had those closest to him inscribe death on the slate of his heart, and listened to the choir, maybe not of hungry children but of starving dreams, while believing that a better day would come. The source of grace for David in his valley is our source as well.

TWO

Does God Recognize You?

The LORD is my shepherd.

Circumstances don't have to change our identity. One young woman epitomizes how the human soul can see beyond and respond to the truth embedded in the crevasses of emotion. In 1996, the same year I graduated from high school, Keshia Thomas was also eighteen years old. The air was sweltering in Ann Arbor, Michigan, in the month of June when Keshia demonstrated who she really was. Klansmen held a rally outside the city hall building. Keshia, an African American teenager, was angry, fed up, and disgusted at the racism and hatred across our country. She joined a mob of around three hundred protesters who vocalized their disgust and emerged in stark contrast to the mere seventeen racists who were there.

In the mystery, we see a miracle happen.

One individual, with a tattoo honoring and promoting the SS, was chased by a group Keshia was in. The group of protesters became violent. The very reason the protesters came out became the very thing they were guilty of. The racist lay on the ground while the mob kicked him and beat him with sticks. But Keshia Thomas, every bit as hurt and angry as the other protesters, did not succumb to her surroundings. Instead, who she truly was broke through. Keshia threw herself on top of the Klansman and shielded him from the blows.[1]

Anger, discrimination, and injustice bowed to the grace Keshia extended. In a world of pretenders, it takes courage to be who God created you to be. A single act of unconditional love reminds us not to use painful circumstances as an excuse for bitterness. Keshia Thomas used her circumstance to call her true identity to the surface.

Just like David.

Sometimes we need to be courageous and be who God made us to be—even when it seems impossible. In David's case the impossibility was because of physical/emotional abuse and in Keshia's case it was because of the color of her skin.

There is a saying in Judaism: the same sun that melts the wax can also harden the clay. The substance of who we are, our identity, is ultimately revealed. It takes courage to see hope when everything within us disagrees. This is what David did when he imagined the words of our psalm. He chose to see beyond the words on the chalkboard and believe the seeds he planted long before would one day bloom. Sometimes, however, it is just so hard to see beyond, and we take on a face that is not our own. Day after day, week after week, and at times over the years, we become someone God never created us to become. We become who we detest. We reflect the very circumstance we abhor. Who we truly are is forgotten.

Sometimes we simply need to know who is near and remember who we are within. We do not walk alone. Like he was present on the ancient streets of Jericho, where the blind men taught us all to see, God has been with us all along. This is the foundation David built Psalm 23 on. He saw God as a shepherd who led him to where he was. Like Keshia, David rose above his experience. He learned to see God for who he truly was, and therefore who God made him to be. In your valley, do you recognize who God is, and does God recognize who you are?

The Psalm Began Years before David Recited It

We know David could not have personally written Psalm 23 in its entirety. Its verses are not written in tenth-century Hebrew, but had been passed down through generations. He is known as its author because it is his firsthand experience and voice, according to Jewish oral and written traditions, that generated what we read today. But who is David? David was a young shepherd boy in Israel. First Samuel 17 records David's entrance into most of our minds when he brought down Goliath. Well-trained soldiers cowered in fear at the sight of the giant. Some fell victim to the mentality that doing nothing was easier than doing something. Only a young, ruddy, unknown shepherd boy named David focused on God's identity in the Valley of Elah. And God brought down Goliath through David.

The streets of Israel, governed by their first king, Saul, were filled with song. Saul's army stood in a valley and saw only death. A shepherd boy stood on the same ground and watched it bloom.

King Saul heard the words of the song and became insecure, fearful, and politically shrewd. Why is it that when a new leader emerges, those who worked so hard and believed so much that the next generation would come then become insecure and toxic? There are few things more dangerous than an insecure leader. David is credited with Psalm 23 but King Saul plays an important role in the story, as he is a primary reason why David will suffer.

Wounds from Someone Close

In Eden, personal stewardship began as God gave Adam charge over creation. In Exodus 18, corporate stewardship emerged as a community of people working together during the emancipation of two million Hebrew slaves from Egypt. The freed slaves became the nation of Israel, and God was their king. But Israel, doubting who God created them to be, sacrificed their identity to the idol of convenience and asked for an earthly king. First Samuel 8:7 records God's words to the prophet Samuel: "They have not rejected you but they have rejected Me from being king over them." God granted their request, and Saul took God's place on the throne of Israel.

When God made a covenant with Abraham in Genesis, he mentioned that Abraham's descendants would be kings. God had in mind leadership and structure to provide stability to families, regions, and nations. Wanting a king was not the cardinal sin of Israel. Choosing to reject God was. When we aren't satisfied with the outcomes in our life, like ancient Israel was, we tend to take God's promises in Scripture and make them fit into our context. When we box God in to what only our context reveals, we dethrone him.

History shows King Saul as an accomplished general. He waged war and emerged victorious in campaigns against not only the Philistines but also the Moabites, Ammonites, Edomites, and Amalekites. But before he became king, we catch a glimpse of Saul's inadequate leadership abilities. First Samuel 9 records how Saul failed his father, who gave him the simple task of keeping track of not thoroughbred horses or cheetahs but donkeys. Donkeys move rather slowly. You have to be easily distracted to lose track of them.

First Samuel 10 records the moment Samuel anointed Saul with oil as he became the first king over Israel. Scripture tells us the very Spirit of God came upon him, and he prophesied. It literally says he was changed into a new person. His true identity in God emerged. This is how the one who lost donkeys became an accomplished general. God can empower a willing person to accomplish great things. Who we think we are and who we pretend to be is never enough.

The same One who chose a prisoner named Joseph to be prime minister of Egypt and the stuttering, eighty-year-old shepherd Moses to be the emancipator of slaves chose the haphazard, animal-husbandry failure named Saul to be king.

The same Spirit who changed him and graced him to lead would one day leave him. Saul would not recognize it. Often we notice God's presence when we are catalyzed in our purpose and experience the favor of heaven, like King Saul. When things don't go so well we accuse God of leaving, only to find out he was there all along. In Saul's case, God never left him, only the Spirit of God who favored him to rule left (1 Sam. 16:14). Even then, God was grieved he made Saul king (1 Sam. 17). As you will see, forgetting who he was destroyed God's handpicked king.

After Saul was divinely chosen to rule, some around him became critical. Scripture says Saul "held his peace" (10:27). We see he had the ability to control himself as a young ruler. However, chapters 13–15 reveal Saul confused his own goals with God's purpose. His first leadership failure was within his heart, for he became a casualty of misunderstanding. His second failure we can read in Scripture is that of presumption, when he offered a sacrifice in Samuel's absence. During a time of complexity, Saul was certain. But he was wrong. Saul's third leadership failure was his refusal to eliminate an Amalekite king at God's direction. During a time of urgency, Saul was indecisive.

Saul's pride, unwillingness to yield, presumptuous leadership, indecisiveness, partial obedience, and insecurity would wreak havoc on a nation and on young David.

In 1 Samuel 16, the prophet Samuel went to the house of Jesse to choose a new king. Jesse invited all of his sons to join him—all but one. As the prophet looked into the eyes of each son, his gaze did not fall upon the next king.

It is interesting to me that Samuel was sent to Jesse's house to find the king, as God knew full well that David wasn't there. David was in the field taking care of the sheep. When it was time to pretend to be a king, David was faithful as a shepherd. David knew who he was and who God is. And David, the uninvited one, was chosen to rule. He didn't have the pedigree, reputation, or any earthly reason to believe God would choose him for anything significant. To David, significance wasn't enthroned; significance was being faithful with the sheep when no one was looking.

And being who you are, who God formed you to be, must not change simply because your circumstances don't line up.

Some of the anonymous, hidden, and often dark moments in life are preparation to sit at the King's table and feast. How we steward our valley experiences and our green pasture experiences catches the attention of a God who, in a moment, can change everything.

King Saul's insecurity over David's popularity turned into hatred. In 1 Samuel 16:19, Saul called David by name to play music for him, and in 1 Samuel 17:55, after David saved the nation from a generation of slavery and pillage during the soliloquy of taunt by Goliath, he forgot David's name. The very one who stood at his side in the throne room and played soothing music, the very one who brought down the giant, was the very one King Saul can't even recognize. Saul, who hid from everyone when he was to be chosen king, was now self-absorbed. Saul allowed his circumstances to change his core identity.

David was Saul's son-in-law. He was manipulated, controlled, accused, and hated by the one who should protect him. Before David became king in the eyes of the people, he learned to worship in the presence of Saul. His enemy.

If you're walking through a valley right now because of someone else's choices, please don't allow bitterness to sabotage your identity. You may have good reason to be angry (Ps. 4:4). You may still struggle to fall asleep at night. You may have to process some of your emotions, erect boundaries, and learn to forgive someone who deserves something much worse for what they've done. In Psalm 23, as we will see, David shows that when we forgive those who deeply wound us we set our true identity free.

When did King Saul change? Scripture opens a window into the king's soul. As they sang of David killing his tens of thousands, Saul said to himself, *What next, but now the people will make David king.* Saul forgot that the people weren't the reason he'd inherited the throne to begin with. God was. Saul allowed the expectations of others to hide who he was. God couldn't recognize him any longer. A life of success and compromise tarnished Saul's identity. Don't allow a spiritual dry season to do the same to you.

David's pure heart before God made him stand out. He played musical instruments in Saul's presence. In David, we see a unique desire to serve at this time in his life.

Ask anyone in Israel who the king was, and their answer would be Saul. Ask God who the king of Israel was, and he would say David. In the moment when the kingdom was taken from Saul, he still remained seated on the throne. Sometimes our divine identity can look different from our situation. There is a conversation going on in heaven we are unaware of. That conversation carries much more gravitas in this life than anything we experience. Saul sat on the throne, but David was chosen by God to be the next king. David's true identity from God took a while to emerge on the earth.

The very one who should have been there to support and protect became the root cause of David's suffering. Right there, in that spiritual valley near the Judean hill country, was a table prepared by God—located, after all, in the valley of the shadow of death. Death is only a shadow. David fled from Saul alone (1 Sam. 19:9–10).

Many of the valleys we experience in this life are not caused by God but by people. David's poetic words in Psalm 23 come through a wounded soul. Other ancient literature is glaringly absent of any sense of self-understanding. Looking within one's self was not commonly practiced, from what we can read. David was ahead of his time. His writing is filled with statements like "I was a stranger," and "I consider all of the works of your hands." David discovered who he was when it was inconvenient, painful, but all too necessary. When the spiritual sun sets and it is dark all around, the breath of God and the heat from his fiery eyes will keep us warm. For the green pasture and the valley ultimately lie within each of us.

The music of this psalm is lost. Only the words remain. I believe it is best sung to the unique tune played as a backdrop in each one of our heartbreaks and mysteries. The motivation of David's heart to begin singing came through an experience that almost took David's life and, even more so, his very soul. As you read, you may not know what it's like to receive a startling diagnosis for yourself or a loved one. You may not understand how depression takes your words away and you don't know how to cry for help. You may not know torment from abuse or the fear of losing a job. You may not know the struggle many face because of their ethnicity or gender. You may not know what pain exists when personal faith is in question or someone close betrays. Or you may.

Your journey to discover who you are and who God is can be that deep, dark place where a word was spoken over you or a bully humiliated you. You've forgotten that when you die, you won't stand before a mirror or your peers to give account. You will stand before God, who calls you close to himself. Here and now, you can peer into his eyes and see your true reflection. Your identity may be the longest battle you've fought.

Some circumstances are not simply a result of "life happening" or "happenstance." Some crucial moments of identity, if we will look back, were carved into the terrain of our minds by those who should have been there to protect us. Like David, maybe you were betrayed, violated, or wounded by someone who should have loved you, like Saul. Or maybe you are the one who caused the pain. As you read, do you realize some do not know their God-given identity—and you contributed to that? For all of us, God is there to restore and make new. And, as we will see, it's in the valley where he does some of his most beautiful work.

Quiet Desperation

David, after fleeing Saul alone, came to a place in 1 Samuel 22:5 called the forest of Hereth (or Cheret), so named because of its barren and dry landscape. The name literally means "baked earthenware." It is a place just like the Sahel, and it is here that quiet desperation enveloped David. King Saul had issued an edict for David's capture. David's life would end if he fell into the hands of Saul's elite soldiers. David was discouraged and surrounded by a clear and imminent danger. He was a fugitive. He appeared to be disloyal to Saul. He fled—not out of bitterness but to establish boundaries. He was also surrounded by God, yet I wonder if David was always aware.

Psalm 23 contains fifty-seven words, the numerical equivalent of the word *nourishes*. It also contains 227 letters, the numerical equivalent of *blessing*. Some Jewish scholars conclude that those who recite this psalm—and, more importantly, live it—will experience God's ample supply, or "blessing and nourishment."

The White House and the Black Forest

The President of the United States has access to some amazing chefs. Being the president is obviously a difficult job. The thought

44

of making decisions that affect the free world day in and day out, amid countless pressures, sleepless nights, and the hope of having accurate intelligence, is enough to make me grateful for my bowl of organic frosted wheat squares. As a foodie, however, who enjoys watching the food channel, I ask to be allowed to drift away into culinary heaven for just a blink.

Waking up in the middle of the night, with a mind full of decisions to make, I would ring the kitchen. "Hello, Mr. President, what can I make you to eat?" Though I am one of the most powerful people in the world, I would probably say, "May I please have a grilled cheese sandwich on sourdough bread?"

"Certainly, Mr. President. Would you like anything else on that? Bacon, jalapenos. . . ."

"Bacon! Of course, why didn't I think of that. I am the president. Bacon it is. Make that slab bacon, because bacon was made by God to be thick. And freshly sliced jalapenos sound just fantastic."

At this point, my days of eating grilled cheese in the great state of Iowa fade as I realize I can actually live out my own episode of *Diners, Drive-Ins and Dives* 24/7. "Mayonnaise. Let's stick some mayo on there. And potato chips. No, a lobster tail, with drawn butter." Potato chips? Some old habits die hard.

"I just made a blackberry jam cake. It's your wife's recipe. Would you like—"

"Would I like a piece? Give me two pieces. I'll eat one for breakfast with my coffee." (Side note: my wife's blackberry jam cake is ridiculously good. I get it once a year on my birthday. I end up eating almost the entire cake. And yes, I can eat it all. Don't judge me. It's just that good.)

For a foodie, being elected to the presidency would have its perks. But when David was chosen to be king, he didn't have access to a chef. No, he didn't move into a castle like the president moves into the White House. Rather than living in the palace surrounded by bodyguards, he knew the very bodyguards who should have protected him had been ordered to hunt him down. David's palace was a damp and cold cave or ravine amid the forest of Hereth.

As the sun set and the cool breeze whistled through the leaves, David would hear a twig snap, perhaps, as one of Saul's soldiers bent down to see where David lurked. Rabbis comment that during this time David was starving to death. Forget about the on-call professional chef. It's not that he hadn't had a hot meal in a day or his grilled cheese was cold. David was losing weight at a rapid rate. He was starving to death. He was about to die.

But surrounded by his enemies in the valley of the shadow of death, the very words of Psalm 23 come off of his lips. And how did he start?

Just You and God

The LORD is my shepherd. Like a helpless and wandering sheep, the shepherd boy turned king refers to God as his shepherd. David recognizes that regardless of where he ends up, he is led there by and with an unseen certainty. His shepherd, the Good Shepherd, is with him. He is led by One who cares deeply where he ends up.

David does not refer to God as his king. In his moment of brokenness, David is not looking for a powerful God to set him free from his situation. He hearkens back to those years as a young shepherd. David was not overlooked by man. No. In those years ultimately he was hidden by God. Sometimes, when we feel alone, God has us to himself. As a shepherd, David learned a lot about God. In this moment, those memories comforted him.

Do you remember those moments with God when it was simple? Before most of your contemporaries and friends questioned the things you were eager to embrace? Maybe you long to get back to the time when God wasn't just your Lord, Savior, King, or Judge. He is those things. Scripture testifies as such. But he is also the One who dwells with the brokenhearted. He stooped down and rescued the woman caught in adultery. He even looked at Judas the night he was betrayed and still called him "friend." He is our Shepherd (Isa. 40:11; John 10:11; 1 Pet. 5:4) and, ironically, though it was not a respected vocation throughout Scripture, he is not offended to be so.

Much of the Bible was written by or describes shepherds. Abraham, who gave us no indicator he was looking for God, was encountered by him and became a vagabond in search of a city whose builder and maker was divine. Joining the throng were Moses, Isaac, Jacob, and David, to name a few. People who were in search of a city whose "builder and maker was God" became used to wandering. The presence of shepherds was a call to pray for their own land to call home. Some Jewish writing says the negative outlook on shepherds began when Cain (a farmer) killed his brother Abel (a shepherd), but only after Israel requested Saul to sit on the throne did shepherding become an increasingly repulsive job.

Midrash "Shocker Tov" comments, "There is no occupation which is more degrading and lowly than that of the shepherd." In the Talmud (treatise "Sanhedrin"), we read that shepherds were not to be allowed in the courts as witnesses. In the treatise "Avodah-Zarah," no help must be given to the heathen or to shepherds. During the time of Christ, shepherds were no more honored. How fitting it is that God drew shepherds to himself when the Christ child was born. David referred to God as his Shepherd, for he knew God's identity and his own.

God identifies with us in our mess. He is not insecure. He is in a good mood. He is pure love. He can handle it when we identify with him in language we can relate to. This is what David is doing when he opens up the psalm. He is going back to those moments in his life when God's presence was felt because, at the time of Psalm 23, God's presence is disguised as God's absence. David did the same that day on the battlefield shortly before he fought Goliath.

First Samuel 17:34–36 says,

> But David said to Saul, "Your servant has been keeping his father's sheep. When a lion or a bear came and carried off a sheep from the flock, I went after it, struck it and rescued the sheep from its mouth. When it turned on me, I seized it by its hair, struck it and killed it. Your servant has killed both the lion and the bear; this uncircumcised Philistine will be like one of them, because he has defied the armies of the living God" (NIV).

Just like David was faithful to watch over his sheep, he senses the same protection from God, his Shepherd.

When you wonder if the situation you're in is too small for God to care about or too big for him to provide for, just remember the Shepherd. Shepherds take a lowly occupation to care for sheep and, like David, this Shepherd can and will fend off even the fiercest of beasts to protect you. The Lord is your Shepherd.

Like the father in the Sahel, sometimes God takes us by the hand and walks through the barren place with us to explain why. And sometimes God runs to us when we are buried so deep in pain and heartache that the last thing we need to know is "why." We simply need to know we are not alone. The road to peace is paved with identity.

Buried Alive

God is willing to overcome any barrier, to dig through the rubble, to walk the long and dusty road just to bring us home. Why? His words to the prophet Isaiah explain further. "I will give you the treasures of darkness." In the valley of shadows treasure is buried beneath the devastation. He is the treasure.

On Wednesday, December 7, 1988, an earthquake shook the northern region of Armenia, 6.9 on the Richter scale. This earthquake was followed by powerful aftershocks continuing for months. The United Nations estimated more than 25,000 people were killed, at least 15,000 more were injured, and the physical damage equaled $14.2 billion (US).[2]

I remember hearing the story of an Armenian man who walked his son to school that morning.[3] Just like always, he dropped his son off at the front door. Moments after he returned home, the earthquake hit. The man waited for the shaking to stop before sprinting back to the school to make sure his son was okay.

As he ran, he noticed crumbled buildings on the sides of the streets; traffic had lurched to a stop. People were stunned. Screams echoed. The city was in shambles. But he kept running. He arrived at the school, horrified by the sight. The school building was in a heap on the ground. Parents and spectators stood around the periphery, sobbing. Time stands still and troubles are fleeting when what matters most seems to become a vapor.

Onlookers, police, and medical personnel stared at what used to be the school. It was unsafe to venture beyond the established safe zone. This father, on the other hand, didn't waste any time. Immediately, he started to pick up the stones and broken chunks of concrete of the building—some nearly as big as he was—and moved them to the side. Onlookers couldn't believe their eyes. They couldn't believe this father was strong enough to remove the stones from the pile of rubble, and they couldn't believe anyone would be naïve enough to think anyone would still be alive underneath.

They urged him to stop. "You know they are dead. You can't help!" they called after him. Even a policeman encouraged him to stop. The father kept digging.

Hours passed, then a full day passed. Still no sign of his son—or any other survivor. The father kept digging. He didn't eat, didn't sleep. All he did was dig and dig until, finally, out of the depths of the rubble, he heard a small sound. He moved toward the noise and kept digging. Within minutes, he revealed a small opening, deep below the surface, where several kids were hiding—including his son.

"Arman!" the father cried, reaching down for his son's hand. "Grab my hand!"

A voice answered him, "Father, it's me!" Then he added these priceless words. "I told the other kids not to worry. I told them if you were alive, you'd save me, and when you saved me, they'd be saved too. Because you promised, 'No matter what, I'll always be there for you.'"[4]

Arman knew his dad was searching for him. Arman was not afraid his father would forget him. Like Arman, we too can wait, knowing who we are will come to the surface with help from Someone above. The Father will not stop until he brings you out.

Sometimes when I tell people my life story and the weight I was resurrected from—that I have come from drug addiction and encounters with demons, near-death experiences, and so on, they think one of two things, either, *Wow, I'm so glad I don't have a story as dark as Heath's story,* or *Wow, I wish I had a testimony as interesting as Heath's.* Either way, I'm afraid they're missing the point.

We are *all* buried beneath a heap of memories, words, re-grets, thought patterns, mistakes, sins, abuses, and mysteries. A weight we cannot possibly lift. We lose sight of our place "underneath"—to lean on our spiritual pedigree or our upbring-ing or our achievements. But no matter where we've come from or what church we go to or how "put together" our life is, without God's grace we're unable to climb out. God is digging through the rubble to get to us, and when he finally breaks through, I pray we respond like the rescued son Arman: *Somehow, deep inside my soul, I always knew you were coming.*

Like Keshia, making a simple choice to let who we are break through the façade of anger, projection, hurt, and numbness can set the love of God free in our situation when our identity in Christ is revealed. We choose to love when anger would be convenient. We choose to hope when a better day is not in sight.

And like David in the forest of Hereth, although you can still hear the echo of the songs sung after you defeated the giant, when your circumstances do not seem to line up with the char-acter of God, who God is to you and who you are to him will be made clear.

THREE

What We See in the Valley

I shall not want.

When our two daughters were a lot younger, my wife, Ali, and I celebrated our wedding anniversary with them. It was an experience we will never forget. Our December wedding provided the perfect opportunity to purchase tickets to *The Nutcracker* ballet as an anniversary present for the family. We got dressed up and carried our two toddlers out on the town for a romantic and fun-filled evening. Forget about limos and candles on the beach! We had car seats and little goldfish crackers in our car. We pushed through the fog from our breath as we walked through the freezing December air from our car to the university's convention center. The facility was state-of-the-art, and we were all eager to continue the night.

As soon as the performance began, the lights dazzled and the sound captivated our two little girls. I must confess that "Mom and Dad" were pretty impressed too. As parents, watching your children smile and laugh at events like this is well worth the money. Our older daughter leaned over to Ali, and I overheard her say, "Oh, Mommy, the Sugar Plum Fairy is so beautiful." Moments later, our younger daughter, unaware that both men and women wear similar clothing to dance ballet, said, "That man is wearing tights!" The intermission provided a much-needed break to stretch and grab some water. If memory serves me right, the girls even had some of their crackers and gummy snacks.

After intermission, artistic expression and a narrative as old as modern society began again. Our daughter, once again enamored with the beauty of the fairy, whispered to Ali, "Oh, Momma, when I grow up I want to be like the Sugar Plum Fairy." Her younger sister, however, at just the right moment when the audience was mesmerized and the music faded, loudly pontificated to us and everyone around us, "Gross, his tights are stuck in his bottom!" The innocence of our little girl, distracted by a man wearing tights that were seemingly uncomfortable, was funny.

When it finished, we left the ballet with smiles on our faces and full hearts. It had been a dream come true for my girls, and Ali and I were elated. It was a great anniversary present for us all.

We scooped up our girls and walked quickly to the car; after all, their cute little legs couldn't move fast enough. It was a bitter and cold winter night in Iowa. With the young girls strapped into their car seats, we tried to stay warm as the car heated up. That's when we heard the sound. You know, the sound any parent is familiar with—the sound of a child throwing up in the backseat. My plan for our wedding anniversary did not include vomit.

We turned around and saw that the reservoir had opened and a flood was in our car. In that moment you are concerned both for your child's well-being and simultaneously planning how many bottles of disinfectant will be needed to eradicate the odor from your vehicle. We attended to our little girl before attempting to clean up the mess as best as we could, then drove home.

Our hearts were still full and we were all still smiling—the car just smelled.

The next day we reflected and shared memories as we went over *The Nutcracker* experience with our girls. It is always so much fun to share memories and talk with each other. Our older daughter encapsulated her experience by stating how much she loved the Sugar Plum Fairy. She loved her hair, her outfit, and her majesty. Our younger daughter couldn't stop laughing at the male ballet dancer whose tights seemed unnatural to her and recounted her moment of vomit. To one daughter, the experience entailed future goals and the whimsical notion of fairies, while the other was grossed out and puked.

Same experience. Different perspectives.

Our perspective is drawn from our previous experiences; our current experience is defined by our perspective. This is true for all of us.

Many people beg the question, "Is the glass half-full or half-empty?" I have a feeling when God hears this, he inquires, "There is a glass?" I am sure the concept of half-full or half-empty is also foreign to him. After all, our cup runs over according to the psalm. God has a perspective we can't forget about either (see Isa. 55:8). Don't believe me? Numbers 20 tells the story of Moses being instructed by God to speak to a rock, and God would miraculously cause water to flow from it. Enough water, by the way, to hydrate millions of people and animals. Moses was angry, and he hit the rock instead. To the people, Moses was a great leader, for their need was met. From God's perspective, this was one of the greatest failures in Moses's life. This act of disobedience, seemingly minimal to us, disqualified Moses from entering into the Promised Land.

What God sees is not always communicated to everyone right away. And just because we do not see, or are unaware, does not diminish what the truth is. What God sees is much more real than what we see.

Scripture is clear: God fills the earth with his glory. He is ever-present and all-knowing. As God sits in heaven and is highly exalted above all, we often depict him peering down upon us. I know he sees within, and I can guarantee he likes to get close and look us in the eyes, but I also understand what God looking down on us implies. We quite often think in hierarchical ways. When you look up, you see the top of the mountain, and when you look down, you see the bottom of the valley. When God looks up, what does he see? There is nothing above him. Yet, in the words of the Hebrew blessing, God causes his face to shine upon us (Num. 6:25). The word picture is God scooping us up in his arms and holding us above himself. What does God see when he looks up? He sees you and me.

To God, a mountain is merely an inverted valley and a valley an inverted mountain. God walks down to stand on top of the mountain, but you and I walk up. From our king's perspective, the valleys we experience are mountains. In Exodus 19, Moses went up on the mountain to talk with God. There, God showed Moses things he did not see before but God had seen all along. God's perspective is more accurate, complete, and clear than ours.

Families enjoy packing up the SUV and traveling to the mountains to see farther than their usual day allows. We take pleasure when we see beyond. It fascinates us when we can see with our eyes what was there all along—just visually inaccessible. I want you to imagine God taking you on a journey to the high place, but this one is inverted and found in the valley. It is there you have access to a vantage point you did not before. You stand with God on the highest pinnacle of your faith, in the lowest of valleys, and see beyond.

What you and I see is not all there is. I am reminded of words T. S. Eliot wrote: "[We have] knowledge of speech, but not of silence. Knowledge of words, and ignorance of the Word. . . . Where is the wisdom we have lost in knowledge? Where is the knowledge we have lost in information?"[1] The modern mind is uncomfortable with not knowing; therefore, we fill the empty space with facts, numbers, assumptions, and media. We grade our children in school on how much information they absorb and regurgitate. We hire qualified individuals with graduate degrees and doctorates because of their demonstration of aptitude. Information is good; after all, I certainly wouldn't want a farmer filling in for my neurosurgeon, or vice versa.

The prophet Hosea informs us we are destroyed not for lack of information but for lack of knowledge. Knowledge says, "This is a hammer." Wisdom says, "Don't use a hammer to floss your teeth." Wisdom, information, and knowledge are gifts to us all and often make life work. What do we do when all these amazing gifts do not make life work? We go looking for something else we can find to explain that which we do not understand.

Though T. S. Eliot's words are vast with meaning, I believe one of his points is this: we easily educate ourselves beyond simple trust. There is a primal longing within us all for a world we do not see. Solomon said, "He has put eternity into man's heart" (Eccles. 3:11). Our final destination on this journey is not beyond—it is within. This is impossible to understand. What if the most important things in life are not intended to be understood? What if they are simply supposed to be embraced? To do so requires trust in a God who sees, knows, and often does not tell us. And that's okay.

There are ways of understanding that govern how we interact with previous experiences and current situations. What we stare at on our chalkboard is absorbed into our soul. The same is true for spiritual realities, especially when we walk through the valley of the shadow of death.

Most of the time, when children abandoned by their father end up in a relationship with God, there are thinking patterns they need to unlearn even into adulthood. A grownup can feel as if God will leave him or her, like that earthly father did, if he or she doesn't perform just right. But when a father stands by the side of his children through both the smooth times and the rough, as adults they typically will be more comfortable coming to God in prayer about both the big and the little things. There are exceptions, of course, but you get the point. The source of our understanding and perspective affects how we view and embrace what is going on spiritually. Your relationship with God in this moment can change your perspective.

Don't Believe Everything You Feel

It is important to note that when you read the Bible, the Bible also reads you. I remember someone once saying, "When you read the Bible, you either read what you believe, or you believe what you read." Scripture is a mirror. It offers a true reflection of who you are and who God is. Scripture is also used by the Holy Spirit to dissect not only right from wrong but also feeling and perception from reality. As the book of Hebrews says, Scripture divides "soul and of spirit" and "joints and of marrow" (Heb. 4:12). We never exhaust the full meaning of God's Word.

In the Davidic psalms, aside from chapters and verses, scribes inserted a few key words that capture the essence of the writing. These were handed down orally for generations and eventually written down. One of two headings is usually added before the psalm begins. Sometimes it will say "Of David, a Psalm" and at other times it will say "A Psalm of David." Some orthodox Jewish commentaries and rabbis explain it this way. Whenever it says "Of David, a Psalm," it means David found himself in the very presence of God, the *shekinah*. From a posture of response, David would then pick up an instrument and begin singing the psalm. They are praises, or *Tehillim*, and meant to be sung. Some psalms are in response to God's presence and identity, when we find deep contentment in our experience of his goodness.

Whenever it says "A Psalm of David," something different was going on in the moment. Rather than responding to God's presence, David has picked up his instrument and begun to sing about things he wasn't experiencing in the moment. His contentment was not found in the goodness of God in tangible ways; rather, his contentment was found in God alone. He wanted nothing else, for God was with him even when his circumstance made it seem like God was absent.

David's understanding doesn't define his spiritual reality. He knows there is more to the *Nutcracker* than he sees. He is playing and singing out of trust in God even when his circumstances give him reason not to. Psalm 23 is "A Psalm of David."

Don't think for a second that David was a superhero who walked into the valley of the shadow of death full of faith and hope and ready to wake up happy. David was a real person with real emotions. There were times when he was terrified, angry, and hopeless, and still he picked up his instrument and began to worship. Like the blind men beside the Jericho road in their unique valley, David cried out in Psalm 23 when he had no reason to believe God was close, let alone going to stop for him. But God did stop for him; actually, God will eventually invite David into his very home.

We Shall Not Want?

The answer to David's cry for help was unexpected. God heard and responded not by taking David around the valley of the shadow of death but by taking him through it. "The LORD is my shepherd. *I shall not want.*" Really? You shall not want? You are alone, isolated, wanted dead or alive, and starving to death. Saul betrayed you and is hunting you down like vermin. How dare you, David! How can you audaciously say you want nothing when you need everything?

In the midst of the valley, David's eyes landed on a lush pasture. It wasn't that the pasture was greener on the other side of the valley, so to speak. It was that there, in the midst of the valley, David saw the rain coming. And when the rain comes, all of the seeds that lay dormant begin to bloom.

Contentment is a unique word. "Godliness with contentment is great gain" (1 Tim. 6:6). That word for contentment, *autarkeia*, is also used in 2 Corinthians 9:8 and is a word Plato and Aristotle used to refer to a perfectly conditioned life, where no additional help is needed. Why? In Scripture, the context is a Christian in whom lives the Spirit of Christ. This reality, according to Scripture, is the foundation on which contentment is built. Contentment is not the absence of desire for more. The psalms tell us, after all, that when we find our delight in God, he grants us the desires of our heart. The word *desire* can mean "of the father." Not all desire is bad. Indeed, some desires are planted within by a divine hand.

Contentment is a spiritual place we can come to when our identity is no longer tied to what we have, feel, or even experience. Contentment is the fruit of knowing who God is and who we are in him. When we lack something, we remain content, for we are invited to sit at the table of the King. We choose not to settle for the crumbs on the floor when we have a place prepared just for us. We are part of a *royal* priesthood (1 Pet. 2:9) and a kingdom that cannot be shaken (Heb. 12:28). Unfortunately, too often we go looking for something to satisfy only to realize that, once we have it, we still want.

I Shall Not Want Anything but a Lawn Chair

The KJV renders Psalm 23:1 as "The LORD is my shepherd; I shall not want." More accurately, the Hebrew says "I shall lack for nothing." In the seventeenth century, the English word *want* meant "lack" rather than today's "covet," "crave," or "need." This phrase used by David is missing what is called a causal conjunction. It isn't saying that because God is our shepherd, we will therefore no longer have any wants. It's okay to want certain things. God is just fine if you want your children to be healthy. He can handle you wanting to take the day off and sleep in a bit (especially if you have little children!). He can even handle it if you want jalapenos on that grilled cheese sandwich we discussed earlier. What David is declaring is that God is enough even when he doesn't have enough. This is what contentment looks like. Even as he wants, he doesn't want. The green pasture is not the source of David's contentment: God's identity is. There is something calling deep within David, and it echoes. God will meet your needs because he is the One leading you into those seasons you will have them. In the forest of Hereth, starving to death and surrounded by life-threatening enemies, David wanted nothing. Sometimes it's okay to want nothing else. Larry Walters would tell you so.[2]

A few days before celebrating our independence as a nation, Larry Walters, a North Hollywood truck driver, finally had enough. Day after day, week after week, Larry had experienced the same thing. Driving the same route, painstakingly and monotonously, he saw the same scenery over and over again. While children and adults alike gazed into the night sky to view fireworks, Larry saw something else in the sky. He saw opportunity. That's when his plan, unreal as it may seem, began to take flight. Literally.

It was July 2, 1982. Larry attached forty-two helium weather balloons to his lawn chair, the same lawn chair he relaxed in after each long week of driving, hoping to catch a unique glimpse of his neighborhood. I can only imagine Larry would've chuckled at the thought of a child saying to his mom, "Those fireworks are so beautiful, Momma—and look, there's a man flying in the sky in a lawn chair!"

I've read elsewhere Larry took along a large bottle of soda, a pellet gun, a parachute, portable CB radio (you know, because it's only polite to let air traffic control know when your lawn chair is coming close), and a camera. He later admitted no photos were taken, as he was simply awestruck by the view.

"It was something I had to do," Larry told the *LA Times* after his ascension.[3] Oh, I forgot to mention—Larry didn't just float over his neighborhood and surprise a few families. He ended up soaring to a whopping sixteen *thousand* feet (that's three miles, by the way) in the air. Larry Walters took flight from San Pedro to Long Beach, and he made decent time (he spent about two hours in the air). The pilot of a DC-10 aircraft spotted him. I can only imagine the passengers thinking the pilot had flipped his lid when he came over the intercom and said, "And outside to the left of the plane is the beautiful surf of Long Beach, California, and to the right is, would you believe it, a crazy man in a lawn chair floating into oblivion."

While he was shivering high in the air, one of the two airline pilots Larry shocked radioed the FAA. Per Larry's plan, he used the pellet gun to sequentially pop the weather balloons in order to slowly descend back to earth. Some of the balloons straddled power lines and caused a Long Beach neighborhood to go dark for twenty minutes. I'm sure that made Independence Day celebrations more of an adventure.

When Larry finally landed on solid ground, he was surprised with a few things. He was fined $1,500 by the FAA, set an unofficial record (because he was unlicensed and unsanctioned) for gas-filled clustered balloons, and gained instant stardom. Larry appeared on numerous late-night talk shows and was offered opportunities to talk about his inspiration in front of many audiences. I've heard that one particular reporter asked him what he was thinking and why he did it. Larry supposedly responded,

"You just can't sit around and watch life pass you by." Larry was motivated to accomplish a lifelong dream. But upon doing so, it turned out to not be enough. At the age of forty-four, a few years after he took flight in his homemade aircraft, Larry Walters took his own life in a remote spot in Angeles National Forest.[4]

Larry had accomplished what he wanted to do. It's an inspiring story about someone who dared to take a risk and move beyond his comfort zone. Unfortunately, this story ended in tragedy, for even someone as courageous as Larry Walters, who served our country in the military, found himself wanting long after he had what he wanted in his hands.

Risking his life for more—although what *more* looked like was elusive and ambiguous—is what got Larry Walters in the headlines. Human beings were created for more.

You were created for more. The fact that you know something is missing, and something just doesn't seem quite right deep within, is a divine invitation to see your life through God's eyes. I'm sure you've asked God why something happened a time or two. God is okay with this. He isn't afraid of your questions, and he is certainly capable of outlining more than enough for you to understand. But have you educated yourself beyond contentment in God? Have you pursued the answer to your question more than pursuing God himself? What if you let go of that insatiable desire and stopped demanding an explanation?

What God Sees

The prophet Daniel learned to find greater value in God's perspective than in finding an answer to his spiritual question. Daniel 10:1–13 provides a glimpse at the prophet's desperation for

God's intervention. During a time of feasting and celebration, Daniel entered into a time of fasting and prayer. Why? His life did not line up at all with what he knew to be true about God's goodness.

At the end of three weeks—a long time to pray and fast, mind you—there was still no sign God was listening. Finally, Daniel received supernatural communication. To paraphrase, Daniel was told, "You prayed and fasted, yes. But, the desired outcome didn't happen right away. There are reasons for it, but let me just say it this way: a spiritual battle is going on with the Prince of Persia." We don't find Daniel anxious. We don't see him concerned. He embraced the reality that God's perspective was much different than his. He was okay with that.

Are you? Are you okay with surrendering to the humbling and fortifying truth that God sees, knows, and is an ever-present help in a time of trouble?

David surrendered to this truth, and it not only stuck with him but carried him through time and again. One of my favorite Scriptures is Psalm 27:4: "One thing have I asked of the LORD, that will I seek after: that I may dwell in the house of the LORD all the days of my life." Asaph knew the contentment found in embracing God's perspective through contentment, and wrote in Psalm 73:25–26, "Whom have I in heaven but you? And there is nothing on earth that I desire besides you. My flesh and my heart may fail, but God is the strength of my heart." In both psalms, God's perspective is acknowledged and embraced.

When we want more, we will go to great lengths, like Larry, to find it. But there is an element in our soul that will never be fully and finally satisfied apart from God's presence in the midst of our valley. We can make more money, be more successful, get that promotion, record that album, start another relationship, even fashion an aircraft from backyard furniture, and still it won't be enough.

There are times when we wander into the valley because of our own decisions. Lung cancer is certainly a valley of the shadow of death, for example, but getting mad at God when we smoke for fifty straight years and receive our diagnosis is hardly fair to him. God is with you even now, and his goal is not to blame you but to love you through it. If you have sought contentment in other ways you are ashamed of, or are discontented with God because of your own choosing, there is grace for you now.

There are other times when we wander into the valley because of the choices other people make. Some of you are struggling in relationships because of abuse you endured and survived in the past. It isn't your fault that you were abused as a young child, and now you find yourself in a deep valley. God is there with you as well. He can empower you to forgive, to keep your love tender, to establish boundaries when necessary, and to receive wisdom to know the difference between suspicion of those who may hurt you and discernment to protect your heart. He didn't bring about the valley. He will bring you through it.

When God looks at your life, he doesn't need something else, like a lawn chair, to make him more satisfied with what he sees. He looks at you and, seeing the righteousness of Christ, declares you are enough. All God wants is you. When you find yourself, inexplicably, in the peaceful and tranquil quiet only God provides, you can say "I shall not want," or "I lack for nothing." The One who says you are enough, just the way you are, reassures us that he is enough in those moments when God is not just our God, or our Provider, or our Great Liberator, but also our Shepherd.

Dark Times Reveal Who We Truly Are

Yes, our choices and the choices of others affect our world. And then there are those times when it is God who leads us into the valley of the shadow of death. We wander there, not voluntarily or because of someone else's hand, but because of God himself. His choices and good pleasure also affect our world. These moments serve as a reminder that apart from him we are never full. We want. This offends our minds, because we wonder how a loving God could possibly fathom anything good coming out of our circumstance. There is something about the dark time that reveals who we really are (Ps. 16:7–11). This is why it can be so scary.

Our identity is exposed in those moments we work assiduously to avoid or ignore. It's not who people perceive us to be. It isn't who we pretend to be. Who we are is exposed to everyone—including ourselves and God.

Notice I didn't say the dark times make us who we are. Only God can form us in those moments. They reveal who we are. When God liberated his people from slavery, he didn't turn the nation of Egypt over to them. Instead, they were instructed to pick up as much as they could travel with after four hundred years of human trafficking, genocide, and infanticide, and begin walking straight into the desert. Away from irrigated farm fields. Away from guaranteed food, water, and shelter. Straight toward nothing. They learned a thing or two about God's love as they walked away from provision in Egypt and toward provision in God. One of the mistakes made by Ancient Israel was discounting God's perspective. They had no reason to want—yet they wanted. God himself walked with them, yet they complained, and a journey of eleven days took forty years. The journeys we take are always more difficult than we first perceive.

The generation of Israel after Moses was led by Joshua. In Joshua 14:12, the very region Joshua asks for is the region the Israeli spies were afraid of earlier. Perspective can either fuel fear or it can fuel faith.

God placed the prophet Ezekiel in the valley of dry bones and then asked him to prophesy. God summoned Elijah, in the middle of a nationwide drought, to go to a brook in the Kerith ravine flowing with water only to watch it dry up. Joseph was falsely accused and imprisoned. There is biblical evidence in all of these instances—and many more—that it was God himself who brought them into those green pastures many of us would describe as valleys. It has less to do with our ability to go through the shadowy seasons and much more to do with our willingness to assign meaning to them. Meaning, by the way, that comes not from our perspective and understanding but from embracing God's—even when he doesn't tell.

I want to be clear: God isn't responsible for every little detail in life. Sometimes we make decisions, and they can have both positive and negative connotations. The same is true for the decisions other people make and their effect on the world around them. Throughout Scripture, however, we also see those moments when God leads his children into seasons they can't fully understand. I don't know if the root cause of your situation is you, someone else, or divine providence. I do know God is fully aware of everything and more interested in you than you can fathom.

Like that cold, wintery night in Iowa when we took our girls to the *Nutcracker*, what you see and understand is always—and I repeat, always—only part of the big picture. When we have every reason to want, and we feel like we just can't make sense of it anymore, it is easy to think God is punishing us. When we are tormented by memories of what we've done or what's been done to us, we can wonder if God is digging up our past and throwing it back in our face. There are some aspects of your identity that can only be discovered in the valley, the wilderness, and the desert. This is when the Father takes you by the hand, walks across the parched earth, and begins to scatter seed, your most precious seed, to point to a better day that is just around the corner. This is when your Father God sits you down and explains that though your evening at the ballet ended a lot different than you planned, rest assured, the Sugar Plum Fairy is still beautiful, and he made sure you arrived home under his care.

FOUR

God's Favorite Place to Be

He makes me lie down in green pastures.

God makes us lie down in green pastures. If you're like me, sometimes it is easy to envision walking through green pastures and lying down in the valley. David knew God wouldn't make him lie down in the valley. No matter how long or steep the valley is, we are to continue walking—crawling if need be—but never lying down. Green pastures would have been a luxury to David, at times even a dream. The forest of Hereth was far from luxurious. With David's life at stake, lying down and relaxing was probably the last thing on his mind. He was barely surviving. But as he allowed God to lead him through the very presence of his enemies, David gained confidence in God's provision and watchful care. He lay down in a place no one finds rest. There, he rested.

I remember learning to lie down and rest when it was the furthest thing from my mind. I serve with an amazing team at Convoy of Hope and Feed One, where we dare to believe we can change the world. Much of my vocational work involves feeding the poor, ending injustice one moment at a time, and having compassion on those who feel unloved by meeting their tangible needs. After all, the word *Christian* should be a verb just as much as a noun. Before I started my work at Convoy, a few years ago I traveled to an impoverished nation where I entered a prison filled with female prisoners. Upon entry, I realized the prison was filled with many other people. There were countless children as well.

The sight I saw when I walked in was traumatic. The living conditions were deplorable. The smell in that facility was indescribable. It was filthy. I remember asking someone who lived in that country who was with me where the children came from. In my naïvety, I assumed the children had been sentenced to the same prison. But I was informed that upon sentencing, the women were placed in a corrupt place. The warden forced the women to pay a monthly stipend to serve their time. Did they leave and work during the day? Or like some facilities in our nation, were they able to work and earn money without leaving the secured area? No. If only it were that. The only source of income, if poor families could not pay the stipend, was prostitution. The children had not been sentenced for a crime. As products of prison prostitution, they had been born within the walls of that place. Many of them lived day after day, running around the small courtyard, while their moms were hired by yet another customer. What a heartbreaking injustice.

When the little children saw me walk in, I remember them running straight toward me. They smiled and yelled. I have a feeling they did not receive visitors like us often. We were there to provide snacks and juice boxes, and had craft supplies to visually share the love of Jesus. Many of them had no clothes and were covered in dirt and feces. As they ran to me, I remember thinking I had to stay on my feet. I was concerned about getting down low, for the children had to have many diseases. I saw some had sores all over them. I'll never forget it.

I was anxious and scared I would get a disease. I was uncomfortable with them trying to climb all over me. I froze. My spoiled Western mind did not know how to respond in that moment, for about ten seconds. Ten seconds may seem brief to you. To me, it was ten seconds too long. I finally got my act together, stopped being an idiot, and realized these kids deserved to be loved, regardless of anything else. I stooped and lay down there on that filthy floor with them. They crawled all over me. They put their hands on my face and fought over who could sit on my lap. I didn't know what else to do, so I tried just being a dad.

I remember when we did the craft with the children. We distributed crayons, and they colored in a picture of Jesus with a group of kids around him. Crayons were a new idea to the children. So was the love of God. The last thing I wanted to do was lie down and rest in that place. But once I realized that my perspective was in opposition to God's, I changed the way I responded.

I have spoken to millions of people at a lot of church services, music festivals, universities, and conferences in my life. Many of these were filled with pastors, leaders, students, and worship songs. I can tell you that out of all of my experiences, my understanding of God's love and his presence was blown not by an amazing sermon or by listening to a well-known artist but by resting in that unlikely place and seeing what love is all about. Those children were the teachers that day and I, well, I learned an awful lot about something I should have known all along. I'm so glad I lay down.

Rest Isn't Always Easy

Choosing to lie down forces us to get up close and personal when, in our busyness and commotion, we become successful at what ultimately does not matter. We are swimming in a sea of opportunities, and often they seduce us.

Sometimes we struggle to rest because we do not receive the provision of God in the duration of time we expect. So we strive in our overconfidence while our soul becomes weary. God understood our propensity to strive, which is one reason why, at unusual times and unlikely places, and in a fresh glimpse of who he is, his essence and attributes make us lie down. He modeled the positive impact of soul rest in Genesis 2:2. If anyone doesn't need to rest, it is God. Scripture says God never sleeps nor slumbers. He never grows tired and weary. God didn't rest because he needed to. He rested before he had to. God did not rest from work; rather, I suggest he worked from a place of rest. Likewise, we don't rest from something. We rest in Someone (Ps. 37:7). From a place of rest, like I learned on the floor in that prison, spiritual truths often overlooked come close to us again. God does not suggest but rather commands us to "Be still, and know that I am God" (Ps. 46:10).

When David said God *made him lie down*, it is less of an action on God's part and more of a descriptor of David's life in God. Because David knew who God was and subsequently his own identity as a child of God, a byproduct of that exchange was coming to the place of rest. This is so important we are commanded to diligently enter that rest (Heb. 4:11). That rest is what is behind the concept of Sabbath or, in Hebrew, *shavot*. It is a noun, not a verb. Keeping the Sabbath is on the same list as avoiding idolatry and adultery. It is one of the few laws that appears in the ceremonial, civil, and moral laws (see Exodus 20:8 and 31:16, for example).

The Sabbath was introduced in a culture that thrived on slave labor, in Egypt, and as the Hebrews walked toward the Promised Land they were well accustomed to life as victims of human trafficking. The Sabbath is much more than taking a break from work. It declares the presence of God and our willingness to humbly lie down, even when it doesn't make any sense. I say this as a good indicator of how important a restful soul is. This is something most of us have struggled with. It does not need to be that way. One of God's blessings to those in Christ is coming to a place of rest where we no longer need to strive for approval, run from what shames us, or hide from what causes us pain.

When David lay down, the ground was far from comfortable. The hillsides near Bethlehem were familiar to David. The ground was rocky and dry and very much like the Sahel. The lack of rain caused vegetation to wither in the parched land, if it could even produce vegetation at all. Often, the only way for the ground to produce during this arid time was for relief to come from the scorching sun. It was there David tenderly cared for his sheep. The shepherd usually spent a lot of his time preparing the ground for the sheep.

The toil of removing sharp rocks from the ground is hardly attractive to any of us. But green pastures typically do not exist unless a shepherd goes through the difficult process of clearing the ground, plowing the soil, planting seed, and irrigating the field. The vegetation must then be cared for and watched closely. The shepherd watches the pasture closely, for if he does not the sheep will travel all that way only to starve and suffer. The shepherd walks to the barren land and sees beyond. The shepherd stands in the dry place and believes it can become green.

The green pastures David spoke of do not merely exist. Only dry and dead places someone once stood in and worked hard enough to cultivate exist.

You may be familiar with the Scripture, "He will not leave you or forsake you" (Deut. 31:8). This truth is repeated in 1 Chronicles 28:20, where it is expanded to say "He will not leave you or forsake you, until all the work for the service of the house of the LORD is finished." We see not only a sustaining presence of God, as he never leaves, but also a finishing presence of God. We can rest, knowing full well whatever is being built will, in his grace, be completely built. But that's not all.

The beginning of Deuteronomy 31:8 says, "It is the LORD who goes before you." God never leaves us, and he finishes what he starts, but he also goes before us. It is God who goes before and cultivates every single spiritual valley and creates a place just for you. The green pasture and the valley of the shadow of death are the same place. To feast in the green pasture is also to feast in the valley.

Sometimes we walk into a circumstance and see nothing but death and shadows. It is there God, our Shepherd, has taken time to cultivate the ground so one day we could lie down. After all, *he makes us lie down*. Sheep will not lie down when they are afraid. The Hebrew language for "He makes me lie down" denotes and infers a sheep lying down and snuggling up to the shepherd. I've personally experienced the love a shepherd has for his sheep while in Israel. The shepherd gets down on the very ground he cleared. I wonder if the shepherd thinks to himself, during those long hot days, that one day he will be able to lie down with what he cares for the most. God doesn't walk away when we lie down. He lies down with us. Psalm 95:7 says of our Shepherd, "for he is our God, and we are the people of his pasture, and the sheep of his hand." I am reminded of something Ali said to me recently: you are God's favorite place to be.

If you've ever enjoyed a moment in life, it very well could be that God went before you so you could lie down. If he hadn't, you would've been too afraid to rest and enjoy. We are prone to wander in our hearts away from tranquility. When David says the Lord *makes him lie down*, he is not describing God's forceful intervention in our lives when things don't go well. He doesn't come to the rescue and scoop us up and away from everything opposed to his character. To do so would require our absence from this world and an invoking of his just nature. Rather, David's words are similar to me saying my wife, Ali, makes my heart beat faster when I see her. She doesn't reach into my esophagus and take hold of my coronary artery and make it move. No, because of who she is to me, her very appearance makes me respond. This is what David means.

David's encounter with God and his understanding of God's identity is enough to make his soul align with hope even when hope isn't easily seen. As we will see, the next verse in the psalm describes the waters God will lead us by. They are *still*. That word can be translated "tranquil," which is a synonym for contentment. The word picture is this: because of the condition of David's heart and his understanding of God, though his circumstances are far from hopeful, he becomes imprisoned by contentment. David is free regardless of his experience in that moment.

What does freedom truly look like? You may picture someone dancing around without a care in the world. I think of the freedom of those prison children who, though confined in poverty and injustice, smiled and laughed while we played on the floor. There is obviously a joy that can never be imprisoned.

Freedom manifests itself in our ability to lean on God and simply rest. Resting in God does not deny the presence of mystery—it sees beyond. It means we choose not to go further; we *lie* down, for we can't afford to walk another step apart from surrendering to our King. We rest when our finances are tight, knowing there has never been a day in our lives when God abandoned us. He feeds the birds of the air and he will indeed supply our needs according to his riches. We still choose to be generous.

We rest when we do not know what the future holds, for we know who does. When you hear that little voice inside you say, *Don't become too happy because, after all, it is only a matter of time before it all comes crashing down again*, ignore that lie and soak up the moment you are in. We dare to dream about tomorrow, for we know it is bright.

We rest in worship, for he is worthy regardless of how we feel. Sincere worship is often the overflow of a heart that has every reason to believe things won't get any better and the presence of God seems foreign. Worship is not an overflow of how we feel. It is a response to his goodness that we cannot ignore. So we turn on some music and sing along as if we were surrounded by a choir of angels.

We rest in God when we come together as a family and discuss what God is sharing with us in Scripture. We do not ignore how we feel nor do we pretend all is well when it isn't. Faith acknowledges the hard ground beneath our feet but also sees the Good Shepherd walking ahead. Long before we get where we are, God goes before us and cultivates the ground so we can lie down, and he is beside us.

The Dusty Ones

Hebrew literature and history attribute this part of the psalm about green pastures not only to David's understanding as a shepherd but also to his remembrance of God's provision for the shepherd Moses. David would have empathized with his hero of old. They shared the same profession as well as each served as ruler among the people. When you read Scripture, do you ever put yourself in their shoes? Those we read about were not superhuman. They were original, ordinary people just like us. Most of them had no idea the details of their lives would be written down for generations to come. They had moments of faith and moments of fear. There were times they messed up beyond compare, and still God took them forward. As David would have remembered Moses and received encouragement, so you can trust that the same God who brought them out will do the same for you.

It was Moses who led the Israelites for forty years in the barren place. There too, in ancient Egypt and Canaan, God cultivated the ground while the Hebrews were enslaved. Thomas Cahill, in his book *The Gifts of the Jews*, notes how ironic it is that the Israelites and/or Jews were originally known as *Hebrews* or perhaps *Hapiru*. The meaning of the word is "dusty ones" from the mountains and deserts.

They were the people divinely summoned to the dry places—not to stay but to sojourn through. Desert wanderers. It was there, in the desert, that God supernaturally provided water and food. God revealed his presence in tangible ways. God demonstrated his desire to be with all of them. The desert did not bring death and dehydration, although the heat was sweltering and the vegetation illusory. It brought divine provision. And, as we will see, it also brought *a table prepared in the presence of their enemies.*

An amazing detail of how God cultivates the ground we will one day lie down in, or inherit, is the exodus. When the Dusty Ones left Egypt, Scripture says they carried the treasures of Egypt with them. Where did all of the Israelites get the gold, mirrors, and other supplies to build the Lord's tabernacle? Egypt.

For four hundred years, they were enslaved to build the storehouses of Pharaoh. There is no way they could have known the very storehouses they were building would one day be full of supplies and treasures they would take with them toward the Promised Land.

It may sound trite, but my heart is sincere: you will never encounter a scenario where God cannot and will not go before you. Even in your darkest hour, God is preparing an inheritance for you. The Israelites lost their children to infanticide during those four hundred years. Marriages were strained. Poverty and hunger were the norm. Malnourishment and early death were commonplace. Was God responsible for every moment of hurt they felt? There we go again! Seeking an answer to something far beyond our ability to understand.

No, the ancient Egyptians were responsible. Yet we see God divinely working it out so the storehouses would overflow. Now we understand why Jesus could say, in John 14, that he would "go and prepare a place" for us (v. 2). He's there, wherever that may be, long before you and I arrive. We must allow ourselves to be vulnerable and hope in God while acknowledging our brokenness.

Imagine what it was like to live in a home where your parents or grandparents had stood on the shore of the Red Sea when God parted the waters. Finally, all of the pain and mystery from centuries of slavery were behind them. The Hebrews walked across on dry ground while the king's guard from Egypt pursued them (Exod. 14). I have read that up to fifty thousand horsemen and two hundred thousand of Pharaoh's foot soldiers were killed that day while millions of Hebrews were set free from human trafficking and walked toward freedom. Moses encouraged the children of Israel to stand still and watch God deliver them. God responded with, "Why are you crying out to me? Tell the Israelites to move on" (Exod. 14:15 NIV). There's a time to pray and there's a time to obey. In your situation, it may be the hour to simply cry out to God and trust him. Or it may be time to use the authority we have in the name of Christ to believe God in faith for greater things.

Moses stretched out his hand over the sea and "all that night the LORD drove the sea back with a strong east wind and turned it into dry land" (v. 21 NIV). God parted the sea. Some scholars tell us the walls of water would have been over fourteen stories tall. The Israelites watched as humankind partnered with the divine to change the course of history. What a remarkable and truly unforgettable experience!

Hide and Seek

To prevent his people from building a theology on how exactly God leads his people through difficult seasons like this, he concealed his footprints. Why? He knew we would expect it to work the same way for us as it did for them. It is easy to be convinced of things God never speaks of. Psalm 77:19 says "your way was through the sea, your path through the great waters; yet your footprints were unseen." He covers his footprints.

If you have children, grandchildren, foster children, nieces/nephews, or have been alive for more than a few years, chances are you have participated in a good round of hide-and-seek. As kids, we stayed up late into the night and played this game in our neighborhood. When a group of eight or ten of us were out, it was always embarrassing to be the first one caught. So if you weren't the seeker, you went to great lengths to remain hidden.

Establishing the boundary lines was always important. Someone usually said, "Okay, we can go all the way down to so and so's house, and the street is the other boundary. You can't hide in cars, houses, or manholes. Trees are fair game." I always loved playing hide-and-seek. I found an advantage when I was younger by hiding from the older kids in the places I could lie down. When I was older, and my strength grew, climbing trees was always the best option. I remember breaking the rules a few times and getting into my mom's car or, even worse, sneaking inside through the patio door of my house and waiting until the ideal time to go back out and win the game.

When, as an adult, you have the opportunity to play the game with children, your strategy changes. When that cute little munchkin covers her eyes and counts, the last thing on your mind is breaking the rules so your preschool-aged child cannot find you. No, you run upstairs loudly so your child can hear your footsteps. Then you climb underneath her bed and stick your leg out just far enough so she can find you. The best part of playing hide-and-seek as a dad is when your daughter finds you. You may not know where God's footprints are, but I guarantee you that your heavenly Father is in a place where he can be found.

You may not know where God is going, or where he has been all this time, but you can find him. As I once heard Bill Johnson say, "God is not hiding from you—God is hiding for you."

David didn't say "I will fear no evil, for I know exactly where your foot was, is, and will be as you lead me." We may not know where God is going or where God came from. What we can know is what David knew when he recited Psalm 23, that *I will fear no evil, for you are with me.* And you don't need to look very far for him either. He's lying there, right beside you, on the ground he cultivated long ago.

Free to Rest

When I think of how someone can lie down in an unlikely place, I picture John resting upon Jesus at the Last Supper. Like me on that filthy prison floor I lay down on, John had no business lying down or reclining in this story either. But not because the place they were in was dirty or diseased. Something unimaginable was about to happen. The innocent Son of God, Jesus of Nazareth, would be betrayed. John was there when Jesus healed people. He would've seen the many miracles Jesus performed and heard the astute, mind-blowing teachings of Jesus firsthand. John gave up everything to become a follower of Jesus.

John 13 describes an amazing moment of freedom to lie down in God's presence despite so many unknowns and reasons to be afraid. You may have some reasons to hold on to your restlessness and doubt. Your anxiety may be the only constant in your life. Living on the other side of your valley can even seem like a fairy tale.

Lie down.

Jesus is sharing a meal with his closest friends, the twelve disciples, and he opens his heart vulnerably. He demonstrates the heart of a servant by washing his disciples' feet. He even washed those of Judas, the one who would abandon him for the price of four months' worth of a laborer's wages in his day. Jesus explains later in the meal that someone will betray him. These words would have sent shock waves throughout the room. Indeed, they did. The Gospel record shows that everyone began talking among themselves, wondering who would do such a thing. Many even asked if they were the one Jesus referred to as the betrayer.

Reclining during a meal was a symbol of freedom. I've heard and confirmed through my research that slaves stood during meals. Only the wealthy, secure, and honored would recline at a meal. We don't know the posture of every disciple during the meal. What we do know is John 13 makes it clear one disciple was reclining. This would have been John. During the revelation of the most troubling news Jesus shared to date, John was not pacing. He was reclining as a symbol of freedom and rest. I remember someone pointing out to me once that John was at the cross when Jesus was crucified, while so many of the other disciples had fled. John came to the place of rest and was able to deal with reality. John believed the statement Jesus made and even asked who the betrayer was.

It takes great faith and freedom to accept the reality of what is going on in our lives and still recline on Jesus. Our rest in him, even when we seek greater clarity for the mystery like John did, is never wasted. I was afraid to lie down in that prison because of what might happen to me. Are you afraid to rest because of what may happen? I was not comfortable lying down, because it violated my mind and all I knew to be "normal." Are you willing to lie down although it rages against all you've been taught and experienced? Do you have spiritual insomnia? Your situation as you read this is not your final destination. God is bringing you through; he will never leave, and he has already gone before you to prepare the perfect spot to lie down. You don't need everything to change to experience rest. Rest is not a byproduct of your season changing. Rest is not given in exchange for a different life. Rest is a place you come to in God.

Rest is a Person, and you are God's favorite place to be.

FIVE

Beside Still Waters

He leads me beside still waters.

Going to the beach with my family is one of my favorite things in life. I have memories of holding Ali's hand and watching the sun creep over the edge of the water early in the morning. The colors in the sky at sunrise were beautiful. I remember drawing in the sand at just the right place on the shore to watch the waves slowly erase our art. Our girls would bury me in sand when they were little and lay in the sand to get a suntan when they were older.

One of the best perks of the ocean is its sound. It's mesmerizing to hear the waters pound over the rocks and fold over the sand. We gather at the shore to watch the waters crash toward us.

Sometimes the water, although difficult for the naked eye to see from the shore, moves away from the seashore toward the sea. This is called a rip current. You've probably never studied rip currents much in your life. I haven't either. What has caught my attention about their importance has nothing to do with water, rips, currents, or even the ocean. It has to do with the human soul.

Panama City Beach, Florida, is a place where thousands of families gather to make the same sort of ocean memories my family has. The waters on this particular Saturday were just right and welcomed swimmers to relax. But for nine beachgoers, including two children and an elderly woman, underneath what they saw was something dangerous. And danger is often hard to see.

A mom watched as her sons, ages eleven and eight, enjoyed the water. They drifted away just far enough from the shore that the mom, Roberta Ursrey, couldn't see them. She did what any parent would do when the two boys became frightened and cried for help. She, and the rest of her family, ran in after the boys to save them. That's when the rip current caught them all by surprise.

Trying to save the children from the strong waters proved very difficult. Soon other beachgoers joined Roberta's family in the rescue of the two children. The current relentlessly fought them; they were trapped and were being pulled away from land, nine in all. Bystanders on the beach saw hands waving in the air and voices yelling for help. Before long, the police and paramedics arrived to see nine people yelling and pleading for help. A police officer jumped in the water to swim to their rescue but eventually returned to the shore. The waters were just too rough.

People stood on the shore helpless and waiting, with no way to save those who could drown at any time, and hoping a boat would come soon, as one was supposedly on its way. Then something rose up within the human soul that inspires us all. One by one, the beachgoers formed a human chain. Between seventy and eighty people held hands and, together, were able to venture into the tumultuous waters and save the lives of everyone who was trapped.

When everyone made it to the shore safely, a reporter was able to capture the following from Roberta, the mom of the two boys: "As a mama, I'm supposed to be able to protect them and do everything, and I couldn't do it that day." She went on to say, "I had to have help, which I was eternally grateful for."[1]

There are circumstances so unbearable and spiritual waters so strong we simply cannot make it through alone. God can help us out of the dangerous waters and bring us back to safety. How? Well, it really starts with the question, Why? Why? Because to God the waters are always *still*. There is a realm in God that transcends our reality. One of the metaphors for this in Scripture is water. Psalm 93:3–4 says, "The seas have lifted up, LORD, the seas have lifted up their voice; the seas have lifted up their pounding waves. Mightier than the thunder of the great waters, mightier than the breakers of the sea—the LORD on high is mighty" (NIV). Psalm 107:29–30 reads, "He stilled the storm to a whisper; the waves of the sea were hushed. They were glad when it grew calm, and he guided them to their desired haven" (NIV).

You will not drown in confusion and loneliness with God numbly standing by. You will rise again out of the waters of affliction, for God is not afraid. And your soul, the very thing you feel is insufficient, weak, and frail, is actually being restored moment by moment. What torments you can make you stronger. What breaks you can have a renewing effect. God will make sure of it, for he wastes nothing.

Let God's perspective of the waters become your own. He leads you beside *still waters*.

Two Rivers

Water is a common metaphor that shaped David's worldview. Even as David lay low in the forest of Hereth, he must have been comforted by the sound of trickling waters. The Midrash says God didn't forsake David, and "He soaked this dry forest with a moisture which had the flavor of the World to Come." In Harold Kushner's book *The Lord Is My Shepherd*, he intuitively sees the connection between David's spiritual landscape and the geography of his land.[2] Kushner cites that some of the great empires in history existed because they learned how to control the water. Mesopotamia, literally the "land between two rivers," saw the rise of the Egyptians, who channeled the Nile, and the Babylonians, who controlled the Tigris and Euphrates rivers. Without water, not only is your thirst unquenched but your very life is at stake. This is why many Hebrews complained and longed to go back to Egypt.

Scripture tells us that, while they physically continued to walk the path God paved for them in the desert, in their hearts they turned back to Egypt. Sometimes we stand in proximity to God but in our hearts are far from him. Proximity is different from intimacy. There was a realm of intimacy with God waiting for the freed slaves just beyond the parted waters of the Red Sea. They had to travel through the waters to the barren place to find it.

What do you do when your circumstance doesn't line up with the God who rescued you from slavery? The hot sun from the Sinai Peninsula beat down on young and old alike. It was hard to swallow and breathe. Why would God demonstrate his love by parting the waters and then lead the people to a place with no water? From God's perspective there was water there. As the people traveled in the desert, God miraculously caused water to gush from a rock (Exod. 17). In a place similar to the Sahel, God irrigated the land. A few million people plus livestock had enough water in the middle of the barren place. God used water to demonstrate the reality of his kingdom that transcends what we see. This moment in time would forever be solidified in the Jewish mind as they would celebrate what is known as the Feast of Tabernacles. Josephus, a first-century historian, said this feast was the most celebrated of the Jews.

During this feast, centuries later, a young Jewish teacher named Jesus of Nazareth would stand within eyeshot of the Temple of Herod and make a startling statement: "If anyone thirsts, let him come to me and drink. Whoever believes in me, as the Scripture has said, 'Out of his heart will flow rivers of living water'" (John 7:37–38). His listeners would know intuitively what Jesus was saying. It was a mystery. It was a miracle. Jesus was speaking in metaphor to an audience very familiar with a God who could cultivate the ground he called his people to inherit by cracking open a rock and causing a river to flow from it in the desert. Jesus said that out of us can flow, not a river, but rivers of living water. What was he saying?

He was saying that wherever we go, because God's Spirit is with us, we can see the valley of the shadow of death bloom. How? From within us can flow rivers of living water. Our hope in God, who is ever near, can cause us to become the rain and watch the barren places bloom. This is how God restores our soul. We learn to trust him and live from his reality, revealed in Scripture, toward our own.

The Spirit of God, within us as Jesus taught, is likened to a river in the context of the exodus. Still waters are not circumstantial: they are spiritual.

God's Spirit is within you, dear child of God. That means God's peace is as well.

In the womb, a baby learns to breathe surrounded by fluid. I think about this each time I read about how Jesus summoned Peter out of the boat to become a water-walker. During his moment of near-drowning, Peter was afraid, and Jesus asked, "Why are you afraid?" Peter probably said, essentially, "I'm drowning! I'm not created to breathe in water."

A few years ago, Ali and I traveled with our two daughters and another family to an amusement park in Florida. We rode rides, ate, and then decided to visit a water park. Filled with lazy rivers, splash pools, water fountains, and yes, hot dogs, it was a paradise of sorts.

We happened upon an area where we could snorkel with baby sharks and stingrays. An avid swimmer I am not, but a proud father I am. The other dad we were with innocently suggested the two of us go swim in the aquarium. So, after kissing our wives goodbye, we grabbed the equipment and began the adventure.

Our families were up above the saltwater tank, waving at us. I couldn't help but notice the twinkle in my daughters' eyes as they watched their heroic father prepare to snorkel with tiny sharks. A voice came over the loudspeaker and instructed everyone. I only remember the phrase, "And whatever you do, please do not swim toward or lay on top of the rock in the middle of the tank. Be sure not to splash or swim in the water. Avoid drawing attention to yourself."

I assumed snorkeling was easy and the instructions were a waste of my time. Big mistake. I paid no attention, nor did I read the steps clearly written at a third-grade level on the large white sign in front of me. I simply placed my gear on my head and waited. How hard could it be to stick your face in the water and breathe through a rubber hose while staring at sea life?

Well, for the average human being, it isn't difficult. For me, it became a nightmare. Do you ever feel like what's supposed to be simple turns out to be very complicated?

The tank was surrounded by what appeared to be rock formations, including a single rock a few feet in diameter in the center of the tank. We were supposed to float, not swim, which I'm sure had something to do with the sharks.

It was time to begin.

Memories of watching Jacques Cousteau on PBS when I was a child flooded my mind as I envisioned sharks and stingrays swimming beneath my stomach. I was ready for this. I was *made* for this. And yet, within ten seconds of jumping into the water, I realized I was not breathing clean oxygen but salt water.

By the way, we were not made to breathe salt water. I became disoriented. Water lodged in your esophagus is not a good feeling. I panicked, kicked, and attempted to scream. I was flailing around like a goldfish on dry ground. My girls' happy expressions turned to panic as they watched the evolution of superhero dad into panicked survivor. At the time, I was a fairly muscular guy, but it doesn't matter how much you can bench press when you're drinking salt water like it's a 7-11 Slurpee. All that matters is oxygen. My only hope of survival (or so I thought) was to begin doggy paddling toward the rock in the center of the tank.

I was in survival mode.

I made it to the rock, ripped the gear off of my face, and held on for dear life. I caught a glimpse of my bride and daughters, who were watching the entire scene from up top. Simultaneously, the same loudspeaker that provided instructions at the beginning began scolding me, "Sir, please stop swimming in the tank and let go of the rock."

Let go of the rock? That was absurd. I couldn't let go. By now, all of the splashing probably guaranteed the sharks and stingrays would eat me. Forget about the fact that the sharks were probably only twelve inches long, and I'm sure stingrays don't eat human beings. There was no *way* I was letting go of the rock. By now my family was laughing at me.

"Sir, let go of the rock," the voice echoed. An audience gathered. If they wanted me to let go, they were going to have to get in and help. I wasn't going anywhere until I felt safe again. Well, be careful what you wish for.

A lifeguard jumped off her stand, covered in red, with her flotation device. She had a smirk on her face. The gentleman on the intercom needed to relax at this point. "Sir, let go of the rock! Let go of the rock! Stop splashing."

The lifeguard arrived at my side, still smiling, and began to pry my hands off the rock. I let go only to latch onto her red pool noodle and hold on for dear life as she pulled me to shore. Everyone stared. Some laughed. Okay, *everyone* laughed. I will go down in the record books as that guy who was saved by a girl in the snorkel tank. Plus I'd singlehandedly ruined the snorkeling experience for everyone else.

A few minutes after vacating the tank, I'd caught my breath. I watched dejectedly as other snorkelers experienced what I didn't. The couple we were on vacation with snorkeled, holding hands and gently wading from one end of the tank to the other, beholding the beautiful sea creatures. As the couple climbed up the steps, dripping wet and smiling, I realized this was my moment and asked Ali if she wanted to snorkel with me. She smiled, and I knew we were in for a treat.

We both gathered our gear and, like any good friend who happens to be my wife, she kindly pointed out, as we stood next to the sign with the rules of the snorkel tank, that I hadn't followed the rules the first time. Obviously, she was right! I paid close attention this time as the voice came over the loudspeaker with instructions. Rather than plunging into the tank and dipping my entire head under the water as I had before, I slid down the edge of the tank next to Ali and entered the tank with my face dry and oxygen freely flowing.

We held hands and I tenderly placed my face in the water as we floated in tandem upon the water. As luck would have it, however, a kink in my hose prevented air from flowing—and I panicked yet again. Did I gather my composure like any other normal human being? No. I dipped my entire head into the salt water again and began to breathe in the very mixture responsible for my first disorientation. Salt water invaded my mouth and lungs, and for all I know was leaking out my toes.

I let go of Ali's hand and, in my kicking and flailing, hit her in the face. Just like that, her knight in shining armor became a little boy before her very eyes. I jerked off the mask and hose and made a beeline for the rock in the middle of the tank. The familiar voice over the intercom announced for the entire amusement park to hear: "Sir, do not go near the rock. Stop splashing. Sir . . . Sir . . . Sir!"

I didn't care. I was dying. No, I wasn't—I was panicking and making a spectacle of myself. I grabbed onto the rock again and held on for dear life. The same lifeguard who saved me before jumped in, smiling from ear to ear, and swam toward me for yet another rescue. I allowed her to tow me again, without offering any assistance as I regained my composure, safely to shore. Ali stayed in the tank, trusted her snorkeling gear to work with the rest of the normal people, and enjoyed the waters. The waters were dangerous to me. To Ali, they were still.

I realized in that moment that I was not cut out for snorkeling—at least until I could have some training in the kiddie pool in my backyard away from other living beings. Additionally, I learned that it was *not* normal to stick your face in the water and breathe. But, like Ali and the many others showed me that day, it was possible.

The grace of God empowers you and me to trust when it is far from easy. I can relate to Peter, as I'm sure you can. I don't blame him for being scared and I don't blame you for walking through the valley you are in right now. Sometimes it's just too hard and we feel like we just won't make it. So we give in to fear and unbelief. Jesus asked Peter why he was afraid because, in that moment, to him the waters were still. As Peter walked on the waters, peace walked with him, for it was within his soul and he knew it not. Even when we drown we are safe.

Well, though I don't blame the disciples for being scared of the water in Mark 4, I'm glad God is sovereign over the storm.

> On that day, when evening had come, he said to them, "Let us go across to the other side." And leaving the crowd, they took him with them in the boat, just as he was. And other boats were with him. And a great windstorm arose, and the waves were breaking into the boat, so that the boat was already filling. But he was in the stern, asleep on the cushion. And they woke him and said to him, "Teacher, do you not care that we are perishing?" And he awoke and rebuked the wind and said to the sea,

"Peace! Be still!" And the wind ceased, and there was a great calm. He said to them, "Why are you so afraid? Have you still no faith?" And they were filled with great fear and said to one another, "Who then is this, that even the wind and the sea obey him?" (Mark 4:35–41)

Remember, not all storms are from the evil one. Jesus was the one who asked them to get into the boat. Jesus invested days loving those he came in contact with around the Sea of Galilee (also known as Lake Genessaret or the Sea of Tiberius). It is the lowest fresh water locale on the earth, sitting about 682 feet below sea level. To the west, the hills of Galilee stretch upward about 1,500 feet. A plateau known as the Golan Heights sits to the east. The mountains of Lebanon, the tallest peak being Mount Hermon at 9,200 feet, are on the north. The winds from the Mediterranean, the desert, and the mountains cause warm and cool air to collide. It is one of the best places on earth for storms to brew. This is where Jesus asked his closest friends to get into the boat.

Those with Jesus had just witnessed miracles with their very eyes. They didn't doubt him then. But during the storm, they doubted. How easy it is for us to forget who he is when our circumstances don't seem to line up. The storm tosses the boat like a wind-driven leaf. For all practical purposes, like Peter on that day when he was summoned to walk on the water, they could all drown. The Gospel records reveal that some call Jesus "Master" and others will call him "Teacher," yet a few will call him "Lord." What we call God in the middle of our storms matters. Where was God when they were on the verge of drowning? Asleep.

Jesus was sleeping on a pillow in the bottom of the boat. How in the world could anyone sleep during a storm like that? Why wouldn't Jesus immediately rise and calm the storm; even better, why didn't he just prevent the storm from brewing to begin with? God's perspective is different. Again, Scripture will invite us into this truth using the metaphor of water.

Knowing full well a storm could come, Jesus asked his friends to get into the boat with him. How audacious of him to sleep. Oh, but remember why Jesus could sleep during the tumultuous waves? To him, the waters were always still. In Hebrew, the phrase for "still waters" in Psalm 23 is *em menu hot*, meaning "waters of rest and relaxation." There are moments when our natural response is to panic, become depressed, give way to insecurity, or hide in shame. But in God's world, the natural response can be to rest and relax.

He leads you beside *still waters* to provide a unique glimpse of how God graciously renews your soul. If you're in over your head and suffocating in your situation, he is there to pull you up. He doesn't criticize you for feeling the way you do. He doesn't scold you for being human. He is there to keep you from drowning. He never leaves you nor forsakes you. He restores you.

Your embrace of God's love for you, in the midst of sinking and drowning in spiritual waters, is how he restores your soul. The look in his eyes when he rescues you will carry you into the next season of life. Indeed, you will never forget it.

He Restores My Soul

The line *he restores my soul* is my favorite part of David's song. I wonder what the melody sounded like when David sang it for the first time. Sometimes the last thing I feel like doing is singing about how, in the midst of deep pain and brokenness, my soul is being restored. I have failed too many times. I have let down those I love most. I have reacted when I should have remained rooted and grounded in love. I have been judgmental of others when I have done the same things myself. I have harbored anger and bitterness when God asked me to forgive. I have only succeeded because God provided the very air I breathe, and yet I somehow thought it was about me. In this beautiful line I can relate most to this king who lived thousands of years ago. I too see God alone as the One who can restore a soul.

David was the one chosen to be king. David was the one who saw the giant fall. David was the one who was faithful year after year, shepherding the sheep. He was also the one on the run for his life though he was chosen. He was not considered capable enough to even serve in the military when the Philistines and Israel stood on both sides of the taunts of Goliath. David's own father did not even think of him when the prophet came to his house to anoint the next king.

After David writes Psalm 23, he will ascend to the throne. His kingdom will be established among the surrounding nations, and the generation after him will soak in luxury and prosperity. Two generations after David dies, his kingdom will be disastrous and his family lineage far from what David would envision. There was nothing in David's past that would warrant God intervening. There was nothing in David's future mandating God would care. God has a way of finding us when we are to bring down the giant and we are invited to reign. It isn't because of us. It is because of what he does within us. God wants more than your success and the things people applaud you for. He wants your soul restored.

99

If David was like most of us, and I believe he was, he may have wrestled with insecurity and anger. Maybe he felt illegitimate. Maybe, as David hid in the Hereth forest barely holding on for his life, he wondered if God had made a mistake. Do you ever look at your circumstances and wonder how in the world God could turn things around? It seems like everyone else gets their divine answer while you still wonder if your day will come.

God cares about your children, your family, your marriage, your dreams, your job, your school, your unpaid bills, and everything else important to you. He is a good Father. You can trust him.

He knows something about you that maybe you have forgotten or are unaware of. He knows the condition of your soul. God knows every single word written on your chalkboard. There, deep within you, everything is related. You have a body, a soul, and a spirit. Who you are is not only your body. When you die, your body will decompose. Your spirit will live forever. And your soul? Your soul is your mind, will, and emotions. When you commit your life, humbly admit your separation from God because of sin, and confess Jesus Christ as Lord, your spirit becomes brand-new. You may not feel new, but if you are in Christ, you are. Remember, you can't always believe everything you think and feel. The "heart is deceitful above all" (Jer. 17:9).

I recently learned the optic nerve, the only nerve going from your eyes directly to your brain, actually sends more impulses from your brain forward than the other way around. In other words, the brain tells the eyes what to see far more often than the eye tells the brain what to see. This explains how two people can look at the same visual image and each see something completely different. This also explains how some people can walk through the valley of the shadow of death and see a green pasture. Our soul is a lens to view reality.

God Likes to Remodel Houses

What happens to your soul? While your spirit is made new, your soul must be renewed. Romans 12:1–2 tells us to renew our mind. First John 3:8 reveals that many aspects of our life are related to the condition of our soul. There are times in the New Testament where the words *soul* and *spirit* are used interchangeably. There are also other times when the word *soul* means "mind, will, and emotions." Mark 8:36 is an example of when this occurs: "For what does it profit a man to gain the whole world and forfeit his soul?" What is at stake when we go through the valley is not our reputation, standard of living, or friendships. It is our very soul. This is why our self-talk and perspective must fall in line with Scripture. We must go by what God says about us and not necessarily what we think.

There is something beautiful about the mess God sees in our soul. For reasons only he knows, he gives us a new spirit but he comes alongside of us and watches our soul become renewed. He likes to fix up old houses. He likes to take dilapidated furniture and restore it. He likes to take people like you and me and reveal his love while we are being restored. And according to John 16, the primary way this occurs is through the work of the Spirit of God. The *still waters* within you, that mighty river, takes the sharp and rough places and makes them smooth.

David says of God in Psalm 23 that *he restores my soul.* David knew his own heart and paid attention to who he was becoming as he shivered in the cold evening in the forest. It is important to notice David said this before mentioning the valley of the shadow of death. One of the primary ways we renew our mind and restore our soul, although in Christ our spirit is new, is to embrace his work in our soul before we need to. David didn't focus on God restoring the throne to him. He also wasn't as concerned about his reputation being restored. David mentioned that God would restore his soul. He knew the importance of the human soul. The human soul courageously walks forward, when you are really struggling, and writes, "But I still love you." The human soul unites with others to form a human chain and save lives at the seashore. The human soul walks through the barren place and plants seed one more time. The human soul is beautiful—and it can also need repair. We can sit on the throne, surrounded by success and wealth, and have a barren soul. It doesn't matter if we gain the entire world if we also forfeit the very thing God wants to restore.

Often, whether through our choices, through the choices of others, or orchestrated by God himself, life reveals the condition of our soul. Like the disciples in Mark 4, we may doubt God's Word in the midst of the storm, though God promised we would make it. Like Peter, our soul may be afraid of drowning, even knowing deep within that God will never, ever stand by and watch us sink.

Psalm 16:7 says "my heart instructs me in the night seasons" (AMP-CE). The condition of your heart serves as a compass. The Spirit of God is at work even when you don't feel him. Your agreement with the truth of God in Scripture may not restore every situation or scenario but it will restore your soul. David says God can restore it. I am in the process of experiencing the same thing David mentioned. For when the human soul is restored, we do not fear the darkness. We run into it.

SIX

Running in the Night

He leads me in paths of righteousness.

I don't know if he arose to the pitter-patter of rain or if the cool breeze greeted him through the window. What I do know is that while others were sleeping or resting, an Indian evangelist named Sadhu Chellappa was on the move. The farther he walked the more urgency he felt.

According to the story James Rutz tells in his book *Mega Shift*, Chellappa was sleeping in a small village to the north of Madras when he was suddenly wide awake.[1] Immediately upon waking, his heart began to pound, and he sensed an overwhelming burden to leave the house where he was staying and run away. Quickly! So he started running.

If someone had passed him on the street at such a late hour, they might have asked, "Why are you running?"

Chellappa would have responded, "I have no idea."

"Oh, okay, well, where are you going? Do you need a ride?" The innocent bystander might have asked.

"I have no idea where I'm going. I only know that God woke me up and told me to run."

I'm sure that would have brought the conversation to an abrupt end. "God woke you up? God told you to run? Kids, stay away from that man. He's creepy."

There was nothing convenient about it. I'm sure Chellappa was exhausted from his trip. When he recounted the story later, he revealed he was used to receiving unique and inconvenient directions from the Lord. Far from straight, his path was filled with random turns. That night he ran into the darkness in remote India to an unknown place. Where in the world was he going?

In the open country, away from the dim lights of the village fires, he passed a large tree. In that moment, he sensed God wanted him to stop and share the gospel. Chellappa did just that. With nobody in sight, he proclaimed the grace of Jesus Christ. In the darkness, sobbing echoed through the open field as the tree branches parted above Chellappa's head. Without hesitation, a man who had been at the top of the tree quickly climbed down and prayed to Christ. When Chellappa asked what in the world the man was doing in the tree in the middle of nowhere, the man confessed, "I came here to hang myself."

What an amazing story of someone trusting the Divine One even when he was hard to understand. And how remarkable that God loved that man so much he woke a perfect stranger in the middle of the night to run to a tree and share a message of hope with him. I'm not sure what happened to the man, but I do know that neither he nor Chellappa will ever forget that moment.

I picture heaven standing at attention while the man climbs the tree with a rope in his hand. The angels are wondering who will be willing to say yes to a summons from God that doesn't make a lot of sense. What would our response be? Each day we have been invited by God himself to take the path leading to the green pasture only to discover it is shrouded with shadows.

We have no record that David went to the forest of Hereth in response to an invitation from God. He may have simply ended up there on his journey. A lack of invitation, however, does not mean God isn't involved. It is my prayer neither you nor I would ever abort a miracle because we fail to walk the path—wherever it may lead us.

Those roundabout ways we take in life are paved with stones God himself lays. God cares about you. Your situation is not a litmus test to prove God's love for you. If you feel like you are in the middle of nowhere, it doesn't mean you are. You are climbing higher and higher in God's purpose.

Walking in Circles Gets You There

Some hills in Israel look like beehives from a distance. Jewish scholars explained them to me when I was there. Circular, roundabout paths are carved into the hills. Shepherds choose to walk around and around the hill to lead the sheep upward. It is the slow path that prevents the sheep from becoming exhausted.

Sometimes we take the long, circular path to avoid danger and arrive safely. The best distance between two locations isn't always the shortest distance. God didn't lead the Israelites on the shortest path out of Egypt toward the Promised Land (see

Exod. 13:17). David would've known this as a young Hebrew boy when he sang about God leading him in *paths of righteousness*.

God didn't lead Paul on the shortest path during his second missionary journey. Paul walked and traveled around 1,450 miles. During his journey (beginning toward the end of Acts 15 and into Acts 18), he often arrived at a location but Scripture records he was "prevented by the Spirit from entering." God didn't reveal to Paul where he was going. I imagine Paul felt as if he was walking in circles. He was. While doing so, he climbed higher and higher up the hill, metaphorically speaking, to where he would eventually gain a better perspective of who God was and who he himself was too.

"Straight paths" or "righteous paths," depending on your translation, literally mean "circuitous ways pointing to or bent toward the right direction." Some translations record it as "paths of righteousness." Sometimes the long way, paved in righteousness, takes us to the green pasture. We would certainly not doubt God's goodness on those journeys. Of course God is leading us! We stand in the place of blooming, surrounded by life and sustenance, and are able to lie down beside our Shepherd and enjoy life. There is also another path paved for you. Guess where it leads? The valley. It too is a righteous path.

Remember the *still waters* from the storm in Mark 4 that blew Jesus and his disciples off course? They left Capernaum for Bethesda but wound up in a place called Gadara. It was certainly not a place where a path paved in righteousness would take you. It was there, after pulling to the shore, that the disciples witnessed how unusual paths do not surprise God. At just the right time, the boat landed so one person who struggled with his identity would find unconditional love. And this one person, who would eventually watch his personal valley of the shadow of death bloom, would make a way for those he would not know personally to escape a horrific disaster from the brutal hands of the Romans around AD 67. Only God can write a story like this.

Only God can write a story like yours. If you allow him.

What's Your Name?

Jesus left the multitude in Galilee only to encounter another multitude in Gadara—one of demons, regrets, missed opportunities, and malevolent memories written on the chalkboard of one man's soul. This was the first trip Jesus would take here.

The man Jesus encountered here, described in Mark 5:1–20, was tormented for years. I wonder what happened to him. Was he a successful businessman who became depressed after an unwise decision? Was he abused as a child and stuck in those memories? Or maybe he was vulnerable and willing to love everyone but was shattered from rejection. We don't know. Likely covered in scaly, leaky sores, he cried out day and night (the Greek word for cry, *krazo*, means "to scream or shriek"). Additionally, he also cut himself—*katakopto*, literally "hacked" his body. As a self-mutilator he was destroying himself.

The people of the region tried to help or fix him. Only their version of "help" was to bind him with chains and attempt to tame him. His condition worsened. A human being with a story and a name did not know who he was. "Legion," as the demons called him, needed someone to walk up to his chalkboard and erase all of the words accumulated over the years. Instead, he was tamed to perform while his true identity was lost.

The world doesn't need another Christian to perform and pretend like it's all okay—especially as we work out our identities as children of God. There is a beauty found when we choose to come in contact with God without a posture of pretending.

It might not seem like it, but we have a lot to learn about identity from this demonized, mutilated, bloodied man. He found his home in limestone caves rumored to be haunted. Sometimes we are unwilling to go to the very places God asks us unless he sends the storm. Jesus didn't need the storm to get there; his disciples did. This man was the least worthy to talk to God. But Scripture records that when Jesus arrived on shore, he went running out to him. Unbelievable.

In this man's day, many young Jewish men memorized Scripture by the time of their adolescence. He, on the other hand, was the antithesis of everything a Jewish man should be. Yet when God himself arrived on the shore, he was the one who came running. Rather than the townspeople running out to greet Jesus, the only hospitality came from a man bound by darkness.

It makes me wonder what this man knew or heard about Jesus that caused him to run toward him. It's probably similar to whatever David heard about God when he reached out during his dark night of the soul. There should be no amount of pain or torment keeping you from acknowledging your need for God right now. His love is undeniable.

Jesus's response is even more amazing. What would you do if a man, covered in pus, blood, and scabs and with no clothes on ran directly toward you—screaming? I can tell you what I would do: immediately look for a Taser. Jesus simply looked at this human being and asked a simple question, "What is your name?" (Mark 5:9).

Identity and Isolation

This, to me, is so incredible. First, I have to imagine Jesus already knew the man's given name. He knows your name too. The second reason I find this question so fascinating is because it gave an incredible amount of dignity to a man who otherwise had very little. The question "What is your name?" humanizes a person, moves them out of "demon possessed" territory and into a position of humanity. With every name comes a story and a chalkboard full of words. In Scripture, names carry prophetic significance and historical backdrops. Jesus acknowledged that this man had a story worth hearing, as do you. Don't ever think he is annoyed or fed up with your heart song. He understands how hard the valley can be and never expects you to just "get over it."

For years the man was simply tolerated. Love, however, is much stronger than tolerance. Jesus simply loved him and asked his name, to which the man replied, "Legion," because so many demons had gone into him (Luke 8:30). That must have made Jesus so angry. It is an injustice for a child of God to live and breathe and know not the image they bear.

The shores of Gadara were walked upon by a man created in God's image. He was a son. He was royalty, and he knew it not. His circumstance and his pain became so normal they defined him. His identity was wrapped up in his situation.

Scholars believe that because of the language this man used, he must have been a Jew. And yet he was everything a Jew shouldn't have been—naked, exposed, hurting, overlooked, and possessed. In Mark 5:10 it was the man, rather than the demons, who begged Jesus not to send the demons out of the region. This was a man so hurting that the company of thousands of demons was still better than being bombarded by the stares of people who knew Scripture in their heads but didn't know God in their hearts. This man was very confused about who he was.

Chances are you've never been possessed by thousands of demons. But I'm guessing you may know what it feels like to be pulled in a thousand different directions. Or you know what it feels like to be so lonely you'd prefer to spend time with someone who isn't good for you rather than go home for one more night by yourself. You may even know what it feels like to be confused about who you are and why you matter. You may have a nice suit and work in corporate America but, like Legion, you still feel naked and ashamed.

People have tolerated you without getting to know you. You understand the pain of feeling like you didn't belong. You have felt like a nuisance, a bother. You've felt like you're in the way. You've felt as if no one recognizes you anymore. In this way, you can identify with this tormented man—having shared the experience of the inner craving for love.

We are all like Legion in this regard. When our circumstance becomes too difficult to picture God near, we perceive his absence. We self-identify by thinking *I'm always going to be depressed*, or *I will never be able to share my feelings with anyone ever again*. We may feel like we will never get through our valley. In this, we call ourselves Legion, but God calls us child.

No matter who you are and what kind of darkness you've suffered, it matters what you call yourself. People will try to tame you and they will try to modify your behavior, but when you encounter love himself, he will ask you, "What is your name?" Sometimes storms blow us off course so we can come face-to-face with the question we must all answer. *Who am I, really?*

The valley reveals who you are. Hopefully your response will be to run to him regardless of your spiritual condition. It only takes one encounter with Jesus to meet who you were created to become. We are transformed in an instant, and miraculously, that transformation continues forever.

In our valley, God comes to us, not to berate us for lying down in the place we were intended to walk through but to look us in the eyes and lead us home. The man's life was changed and his identity restored on the shores of Gadara. In that dry and arid place, his world bloomed. And none of this would have happened if the storm hadn't blown Jesus and his disciples off course. But this was only the beginning.

There is something unearthed deep within our soul when we see who we really are and who God really is. We do not perform for it nor do we strive to have it. A byproduct of encountering Jesus is identity. A byproduct of identity is a restored soul.

Growing in our relationship with him—as we slow down and listen to his voice, turning to see—we discover just how sacred the ground is.

Identity and Impact

In the latter part of Mark 6, Jesus traveled back to the region where he first encountered Legion. His reception this time was significantly different. In the same region where the people had begged Jesus to leave (Luke 8:34), they now lined up their sick for Jesus to heal them. Why the change? The man they called Legion had shared what Jesus said and did to him. We don't know his given name, but we do know the effects of his life after meeting Jesus. Some of eternity's most profound moments go unannounced here on earth. A man whose identity was restored by Jesus brought the kingdom to earth for many.

Approximately thirty-five years after Jesus died, the Romans came to sack Jerusalem. Frustrated and fed up with the Zealots, recurring rebellion, and the growing popularity of the Way (what Christianity was originally known as), Rome would have no more. AD 67 brought with it trepidation and fear among the hills of Jerusalem. The Jews and Christians would either remain in Jerusalem and face murder or persecution or, to spare their children, flee to the surrounding regions.

The early Christians were refugees and sought help from sympathetic neighbors. Unfortunately, many families were turned away at the gates of the cities, for everyone knew to shelter a Christian was to wish death upon themselves. They had nowhere to run, except one place: Gadara.

The Gadarenes would've turned them away too, had it not been for a group of Jesus followers in the area. That group had found their genesis on the roads that day when Jesus passed by and healed many. How did they hear about Jesus? The man called Legion had the courage to remain in a place he didn't want to be, simply because God asked him to remain. Who would have thought the valley of the shadow of death in AD 30 would be a green pasture in AD 67?

We are part of a greater story. God declares the end from the beginning (Isa. 46:10). Even as we walk in circles, we are being led by our Good Shepherd. We climb higher and higher to catch a unique perspective. Not only do difficult circumstances reveal who we truly are, what our "name" is, but they also reveal who God truly is. It is for *his name's sake*. We have nothing to fear. We can lie down in what is now our green pasture and listen to the peaceful sound of the still waters. Our soul is restored, and often it's after the storm breaks on the horizon. He remains profoundly with us, whether or not we realize it.

Frankly, some of us don't. We don't realize the nearness of God nor do we recognize how subtly the landscape of our faith changes. We slowly wander into spiritual valleys at times and all too often are caught by surprise. I wonder if Legion fully understood the valley he was in. I wonder if he ever caught a glimpse of the slow fade in his identity.

There are those reading this book right now who readily admit the valley they are in, whether it is by their own decisions, the decisions of others, or God's sovereign design. All three of these catalysts into the valley come and go, and it is a challenge to understand where one ends and the other begins. The reason for our valley is the least thing on some minds. People just need hope that one day things will change. What happens, however, when you are in your spiritual valley and you don't know how you arrived, how to get out, or even where you are to begin with? This is where God sends people who literally become the answer to our prayers to help. And that's what happened to me.

I Was Legion

Of all individuals we encounter on the pages of Scripture, I can relate to Legion the most. I grew up very aware of the spiritual world. As a young boy, I was fascinated with religion, philosophy, science, and the supernatural. I stood out as a kindergartener when I mentioned Albert Einstein to my teacher. Believing in a spiritual world was not a stretch for me; indeed, as a child I saw more in a given weekend than most do in their lifetime.

Subtle experiences with the occult quickly led me down a road I never intended to travel. Before I knew it, like Legion I was tormented and broken.

I was taught how to consult with spirits by those closest to me. I saw things, things you never forget but desperately wish you could. The most sensational experiences have never been shared publicly nor will they ever be. I remember watching candles float off tables and moving chairs across the room with a glance. Struggling with whether or not a reality beyond my sight existed was never the issue: honing in on the correct and true language to identify what lay beyond was. So I delved into religious literature and studied.

I remember looking at a variety of streams of literature. Hinduism, witchcraft, Buddhism, and a host of other genres captured my attention. I was a good student who made the honor roll, well liked and popular at school, a decent athlete—tormented by night terrors, haunted by my experiences, regularly in pain from ulcers due to anxiety, and oblivious to what normal life looked like. I had my share of hurts, pains, dysfunctions, and memories that fed into my torment.

I want to be clear, however, that the choices I made were my own. We are a product of our shared experiences and thoughts, this is true, but I refuse to use anyone else and the decisions they make as my scapegoat for how I ended up. At the end of the day, we ultimately choose the path we take, regardless of how much help or lack thereof we have from those closest to us.

In eighth grade, I looked like I had it together on the outside. On the inside, I was captive to torment and spiritually dead. That's when a particular girl heard it—or, more accurately, heard him. *You see that boy over there at the locker? Pray for him, I have a call on his life. You are going to marry him one day.* I had no idea what she heard, but I can assure you that the subtle and still small voice, speaking about me, knew all too well what he was saying.

At this time in my life, I took a hiatus from the dark things and gave faith in God a try. Some circumstances in my family created an opportunity to enroll in some Wednesday evening classes to learn about God and religion. This period of time gave my heart and mind a break from the spiritual toxins I was exposing myself to. It was just in time to see something amazing and beautiful right in front of me. That young girl who dared to believe what was communicated to her in the hallway of middle school became someone incredibly special to me.

We struck up a relationship and became close. I remember going to her home and eating her mom's macaroni and cheese. She came and watched me play basketball. We watched the Olympics together in her living room. She was just perfect in every way to me. But when our eighth-grade year ended, we went our separate ways and formed our own indigenous friend groups. Her choices took her down the path of cheerleading, popularity, and attending church. My choices led me toward substance abuse, the occult, violence, and rage.

Throughout the first three or so years in high school, we made contact from time to time. There was always something special about her. Even at a young age I remember thinking I would marry her one day. We actually discussed it at age fourteen. Some called it puppy love. There are things those younger than us can understand long before life talks us out of them. Nonetheless, my lifestyle caused me to come to a desperate place.

One day in high school physics class, while I was hallucinating on LSD, we calculated velocity while dropping shiny metal balls down a ramp. I struck up a conversation with my lab partner.

As always, the conversation quickly turned toward religion and philosophy. Deep inside us all is a longing to encounter the One whose image we are carved from and carved into by his breath.

I talked about the end of the world, how to know what religion was the correct one, and probed and prodded with my physics partner as I desperately sought to catch a glimpse of truth. I was invited to church one day, and, would you believe it, I went. That one experience didn't change my life. But it planted a seed, and God sent the rain.

After weeks of wrestling with what I knew to be true in my heart, though I had no knowledge of who Jesus of Nazareth was nor had I ever really read the Bible, I encountered the One who prepares a table for us even in the presence of our enemies. Like Legion, I was ashamed, tormented, and isolated, but I saw something beautiful in the face of Jesus, though he seemed so far away. Like Legion ran to Jesus on the shores of Gadara, I ran to him in my bedroom on a Sunday evening after the effects of some crystal methamphetamine wore off.

I lay in bed with my eyes wide open. My mind raced, thinking about who God was and what the truth could be. I remember it like it was yesterday. At the risk of doing God's love injustice by limiting it to words, I will try to explain what happened next. It was almost as if the sky opened up and, for the first time in my life, I sensed real and pure love. The first words out of my mouth were, "Jesus, you are who you say you are." There are a lot of options available to anyone who wants to dabble in falsehood. For those who seek truth, love isn't too far away. They coincide, as both love and truth are not concepts, emotions, or experiences: they are a Person.

What I encountered that night in my room took my breath away. In my naïvety I thought speaking with God required bending a knee, closing my eyes, and folding my hands beside my bed. So, after school and work concluded the next day, I couldn't wait to get home and continue what I had experienced the entire night before. For three nights I stayed awake and spoke with God like a friend. I am sure I used some swear words and said some unusual things. Jesus wasn't offended. He just wanted to be with me.

He just wants to be with you too.

In the midst of my darkest hour of the soul, when day after day I exchanged the truth of God for a convenient lie, God invited me to his table to feast.

Trying to clean up ourselves emotionally and spiritually before we come is unnecessary. Come as you are.

A few days after my surprise encounter with Love, I wandered into a little church on a Wednesday night. It doesn't take a lot of bells and whistles to bring about a positive change in someone's life. I am living proof of that. It is important that we don't use relevance as an excuse to compromise, nor should we use holiness as an excuse to create a subculture to hide in. I wandered into what could be described as one of the most irrelevant, dysfunctional church experiences you can fathom.

As a seventeen-year-old, not having slept in four days, with black rings around my eyes and a large marijuana leaf on my tie-dyed shirt, I walked into a little room at that church. There were about twenty or twenty-five people sitting in a circle. There was no worship music playing or pastor preaching. People were crying and talking, some were shouting, and the police were there. I knew one of them by name, for Officer Willie used to search my car on the weekends. It was nothing that church should be.

I found out that evening they were having a "family meeting" because one of the congregants had made threats against the pastor. For safety reasons, a family was asked to leave the church. They were explaining to the youth group why the family, which included two teenagers, would never be back. People were crying, angry, and devastated, and the cops had been called. I felt right at home.

God knows us well. Had I walked into a perfect church building, sat in a perfect pew, listened to the mesmerizing serenade of a skilled choir, and heard a preacher pontificate in Christianese, I would have felt out of place. Here, I resonated with others who saw the need for God to be present even in the dark times. Remember my physics partner? Well, his dad was a volunteer at the church, and that evening he closed the night in prayer.

That's the evening I took a risk and asked Jesus to love me just the way I was. He did. I am thankful I did not allow the uniqueness of my path to talk me out of his true identity. The lack of perfection in the church did not seduce me into thinking God was the same. Have you been wounded by someone or something in the name of God? Has your painful situation occurred under the shadow of a steeple? If so, God is not responsible.

Our insecurities thrive when we look to ourselves for solutions and explanations or look to others to blame. When we look to him, we will see a divine hand that can write our story. It is for his name's sake that he restores you, for you bear his image.

Sadhu Chellappa saw God at work in that small Indian village, even when it was difficult to understand. David and Legion too saw God working when their path was difficult to understand. God is at work in your life regardless of your feelings. He is going to reveal who he truly is to you in a place that does not line up with his character. Though you see a circular path in front of you, the top of the mountain is near.

SEVEN

Pieces and Lids

*Even though I walk through the valley of the
shadow of death, I will fear no evil.*

Something happens in David's psalm when he wanders
out of the green pasture and into the valley. Something
profound.

David is able to capture in essence the shrinking distance
between himself and God. In the first half of the psalm, when
David enjoys the green pasture, he describes his relationship with
God in terms of "I" and "he." It is in the green pasture where "he"
makes us lie down and "he" leads us. When the lush landscape,
once covered with green, is swallowed up in the darkness, literally
the deep darkness, or *tzalamut*, "he" becomes "you." *Even though I
walk through the valley of the shadow of death, I will fear no evil, for
you are with me.* David says *"Your* rod," and *"You* prepare a table."
The language used to describe God no longer depicts absence

but presence. God is right there when you don't expect it and least deserve it. That's who he is. Your feelings and legitimate pain and concern are not your final resting place: God is. There is a realm of intimacy with God that is solely reserved not for the green pasture but for the valley.

What If Our Lid Was Switched?

When I was young, one of my very favorite places to visit was my grandmother's house. On Saturdays, as the tradition went, I would go over to Ma's house (as I called her), and she would pour me a glass of ice cold Coke. I was always amazed at how she could fit just a *few* more drops into my Styrofoam cup without it ever spilling over. It seemed like magic.

Along with our Coke, she would open a package of oatmeal cookies—you know the kind, the hard ones with that thin layer of icing on top similar to the texture of Elmer's glue. We would sit around and eat cookies and drink cold Coke, or hot coffee. The cookies did *not* taste good, but they didn't have to. They were the perfect accompaniment to my beverage of choice. And in the first grade, treats like this seemed perfect.

Ma was obsessed with Scrabble and puzzles. After breakfast, we would always go to Dahl's Foods, and she would meander up and down the aisles looking for cat food to feed the stray cats in the neighborhood. The list was the same every time—Purina cat food, the infamous oatmeal cookies, Coke, deviled ham, and every now and then she'd splurge on a melon.

Ma selected her melons with a religiosity like you've never seen. She would pick up a melon, spank it numerous times, and shake it. Then she'd hold it up to her ear and listen. To this day,

I'm not sure what she learned when she held that melon up to her ear, but she always seemed very concerned about getting the right one.

After returning from the store, we would unload the groceries, do some yard work, and then venture into the house for some more Coke, deviled ham sandwiches, and cookies. We rarely sat at the kitchen table for our treats. That was the place where Ma did her puzzles, and puzzles trumped family mealtime any day.

For weeks, Ma would labor intensely, putting together a jigsaw puzzle (she always bought the big ones with something like 6,000 pieces) only to finish and throw it away. Then inevitably she would pick up another one at Dahl's. I always noticed her routine: the new puzzle was unearthed from the cellophane, the box lid was taken off, and all the pieces were dumped on the table and flipped right side up. She would then prop the lid of the box against the wall and proceed to find the four corners. "Branded by Milton Bradley" was always in the upper right-hand corner. A freebie.

Once the four corners were in place, Ma would begin to build the puzzle by finding the edge pieces first. She would complete the frame and start to fill in the pieces at every appropriate spot—all based on the picture on the puzzle lid.

In other words, that lid was her map. Every action was prescribed by and tethered to what the lid commanded. "Don't you dare put that piece of goldenrod there," the lid seemed to say to her. "You need a turquoise piece instead."

As a child I remember thinking, *What would happen if I switched the lid?* I wondered if she could even continue her puzzle building without the correct compass in place. Of course my wondering led to, one day, testing my experiment—which then led to one of only two times in my life Ma ever spanked me. It's amazing how hard a grandma can hit when you mess with her puzzles. (And don't be fooled by her age. That woman had a pretty good arm on her. Must have been from all that time spanking melons!)

I can't say I blame her. Especially now, looking back, I can see how difficult it would be to build a puzzle from the wrong picture. All the pieces you think should be there aren't. All the pieces you do have don't seem to match the image in front of you. Everything is confused. Everything seems upside down. Nothing makes sense.

Thinking about my grandmother with her confused puzzle makes me wonder about you and me. How many of us are standing in the green pasture but constructing it from a switched image? Does it look like a valley? Think about it for a minute. Does your circumstance become the lens through which you embrace Scripture, or do you embrace who God is, revealed in his Word, regardless of your experience?

When assembled, David's puzzle pieces depicted a place in bloom regardless of what the lid looked like. The words *even though* are significant in the psalm. It's one thing to think you're in the valley when you're really in the pasture. It's another thing to think you're in the pasture when you're really in the valley.

David isn't in denial. He isn't naïve. He recognizes full well he is in a valley, but just as soon as he does, "he" becomes "you," and the God who seemed off in the distance is now gazing right into David's face. God's absence is a bygone assumption. God himself is at hand.

As David looked close enough, I can imagine he saw the reflection of the table prepared just for him, in the presence of his enemies, right in God's eyes. I am glad David didn't lie down in the valley. He kept walking. I wonder how long he had to walk until he encountered God there.

Delight or Desert?

For a plant, drought can be very dangerous; however, at the right time in a plant's life, it can strengthen the roots for an extended period of growth later on. The same is true for your spiritual dry seasons. In the previous chapter, we looked at how we discover who we truly are in the valley. As the language shifts in the psalm, we also discover who God is. We can *fear no evil*, knowing God is with us.

Often we wander into circumstances where our enemy seeks to convince us we aren't who God says we are and God isn't who he says he is. He wants to switch our lid. It happened in the Garden of Eden. *Eden* means "delight" in Hebrew, the language the story of Genesis was originally recorded in. Ironically, *Eden* means "desert" in Sumerian. The same word, *Eden*, means delight or desert, simply based on your perspective and worldview. Adam and Eve were standing in a delight until someone else convinced them it was a desert. Adam and Eve allowed their lid to be switched by the serpent. Jesus of Nazareth didn't.

Adam and Eve walked with God and had the distinct privilege of delighting in his presence. But they listened to the serpent of old and, tragically, their delight became a desert. Satan came and initially sought to bring doubt on who God is (see Gen. 3:1).

His second attack on identity was not on God but on them, and is recorded in Genesis 3:5: "You will be like God." Satan convinced them that if they ate the fruit from the tree they would then—and only then—become like God. What Adam and Eve ignored is that they were already like God, created in his image. "God isn't who he says he is and you aren't who he says you are," the devil said. The result? Death and sin entered the world.

Adam and Eve didn't become naked after the fall. They became ashamed of their nakedness. Genesis 3:5 says the enemy thought Adam and Eve could be "like God." Obviously, Satan views God as naked and ashamed. He has that much disdain for the One who died for us.

Cowering and isolated after shame engulfed them, they heard God walking in the garden (v. 8). I once heard Erwin McManus describe it this way: not only did they know the sound of God's voice but they also knew the sound of God's steps. And they hid from him. God's response? To clothe them. The first thing God addressed was not death and sin entering the world. The first thing on his heart was their shame. What a loving Father he is! In Genesis 3 he is concerned first and foremost with Adam and Eve listening to anyone other than him as it pertained to their identity.

Toward the end of the chapter, we see that God placed a flaming sword to guard, not the garden or the tree of the knowledge of good and evil, but the tree of life. Contrary to popular opinion, this wasn't an act of punishment. It was an act of mercy. God knew that if they ate the fruit from the tree of life they would remain eternally ashamed and disconnected from their identity. God designed them for more. Adam and Eve were in the garden with God only to assume he wasn't enough. Their delightful garden turned into a desert and their pasture into a valley.

The valley of *tzalamut* is used in Jeremiah 2:6 in the Interlinear Bible to describe a place where no one has been before. I picture large sand dunes in the desert like you see in National Geographic without one footprint or tire track. God is with us in the pathless desert, for he has traversed it before. This is why *Even though I walk through the "pathless desert," I will not fear.*

Jesus modeled how to take a desert and watch it bloom into a garden. It is that pathless desert he walked into, for no one could dare walk that path before him. The prophet Isaiah foretold of the day when a way for God would be made in the desert rather than the green pasture (Isa. 40:3–5). In the words of Jeremiah 33:12, "In this place that is waste, without man or beast, and in all of its cities, there shall again be habitations of shepherds resting their flocks." God's lid never gets switched.

With no one else around, Jesus knew he was not alone. He encountered the same deceiver Adam and Eve did in the garden, Lucifer, who sought to afflict Jesus with torment and temptation. His situation in no way communicated to anyone that he was heaven's royalty. How could one appearing to be so weak have a Father so strong? When tempted to forget his true identity, Jesus drew strength from Scripture. Is it really enough to go to Scripture in these moments?

Yes.

The apex of your spiritual battle has nothing to do with your issue at hand and everything—and I mean everything—to do with identity. This emboldens even the weakest one to say *even though I walk*. With the enemy drawing near, would God lie down in the valley or keep walking?

Knowing who you belong to can be enough.

Remember Who You Are in the Desert

Max Lucado, in *No Wonder They Call Him the Savior*, tells the story of Maria and her daughter Christina.[1] Longing to leave her poor Brazilian neighborhood, Christina wanted to see the world. Discontent living at home with only a pallet on the floor, a washbasin, and a wood-burning stove, she dreamed of a better life in the city. One morning she ran away to Rio de Janeiro, breaking her mother's heart. Her mother knew what life on the streets would be like for her young, attractive daughter, so Maria quickly packed to go find her.

On her way to the bus stop, Maria went to a drugstore to get one last thing—pictures. She sat in the photo booth, closed the curtain, and spent all the money she could on pictures of herself. With her purse full of the small black-and-white photos, she got on the next bus to Rio. Maria knew Christina had no way of earning money. She also knew that her daughter would be too stubborn to give up. Maria began her search. Bars, hotels, nightclubs—any place with a reputation for streetwalkers or prostitutes. At each place she left her picture taped on a bathroom mirror, tacked to a hotel bulletin board, or fastened to a corner phone booth. On the back of each photo she wrote a note.

It wasn't too long before Maria's money and pictures ran out, and she had to go home. The tired mother cried as the bus began its long journey back to her small village.

A few weeks later, Christina was coming down the stairs in a seedy hotel. Her young face was tired. Her brown eyes no longer danced with youth but spoke of pain and fear. Her laughter was broken. Her dream had become a nightmare. A thousand times she had longed to trade all those countless beds for her secure pallet. And yet the little village seemed too far away. As she reached the bottom of the stairs, her eyes noticed a familiar face. She looked again, and there on the lobby mirror was a small picture of her mother. Christina's eyes burned and her throat tightened as she walked across the room and removed the small photo. On the back, Maria had written this: "Whatever you have done, whatever you have become, it doesn't matter. Please come home."

And Christina went home.

Her identity, regardless of what she did or where she was, was still that of a child. She belonged to someone who loved her, and that was enough to bring her back to where her value was known. We belong to Someone too, whether we are in the valley because of our own choices, the choices of others, or because of God's sovereignty and wisdom beyond our understanding.

Jesus knew who he belonged to. When the voice of doubt spoke to him in the pathless desert, the voice of truth from Scripture thundered. Unlike Adam and Eve, who exchanged truth for a believable lie, Jesus drew his identity from the reliable Father and his Word. We learn from our Savior how we can stay strong when our greatest enemy lies to our face. Oh, but he is forced to watch us feast at the table God prepares, if we will turn and see.

It was in the desert that Isaiah 40 speaks of where John the Baptist, the cousin of Jesus, baptized the Son of God. Scripture says the heavens were opened and the Holy Spirit descended upon Jesus in the form of a dove. The Father spoke identity over him. Before Jesus performed a miracle or launched his public ministry, the Father was well pleased in his Son. God's words were anchored in identity and not appearance, vocation, or talent. "This is my beloved Son, with whom I am well pleased" (Matt. 3:17). Throughout the Gospels, Jesus referred to himself as the Son of God or Son of Man, never anything else. The identity God provided became his identity. We will see, just like Adam and Eve, that identity will be tested. Where? The wilderness.

Jesus was led by the Spirit into the desert (4:1) to be tempted. He wasn't led by a wrong decision. Satan did not confuse Jesus and cause him to wander off the path. He was in the pathless desert, the valley of the shadow of death if I may, because the Spirit of God led him there. Jesus was hungry, for he fasted for forty days (v. 2). Almost starving, like David in the Hereth forest. It was there, when Jesus appeared to be alone and vulnerable, that the enemy came. Satan would personally come and tempt Jesus. Three times his tactic was to get Jesus to validate his identity in any other way besides simply believing what God spoke over him. "If you are the Son of God, command these stones to become loaves of bread" (v. 3). "If you are the Son of God, throw yourself down" (v. 5). "All these I will give you, if you fall down and worship me" (v. 9).

Satan used the very words the Father declared over Jesus against him. Make no mistake; there is a reason he said, "If you are the Son of God." Satan was there when the heavens parted and God spoke over his Son. The third temptation had to do with worship—but also had everything to do with identity. It's almost as if Satan was saying to himself, *If I can't get Jesus to doubt who he is, then I will try to get him to doubt who God is.* Sound familiar? It's the same strategy he employed in the Garden of Eden, that garden of delight or desert, depending on your perspective. Worship is an overflow of identity. When we know who we truly are, we can come before God and worship him for who he truly is. Not for what he does or doesn't do. For who he is. There is a reason why, when we come into right relationship with God, we are "adopted" into his family (Colossians 1). We are already sons and daughters but only then become aware of it.

Another Garden

In the wilderness, Jesus was hungry and vulnerable yet full of the Holy Spirit when he entered (Luke 4:1). Jesus made spiritual deposits so that, in the day of difficulty, he wouldn't wear down.

Satan eventually leaves and waits for an opportune time (v. 13) to come again. This opportune time would emerge when Jesus would find himself another wilderness, not a physical one, but a spiritual one. Sometimes those are the most difficult to navigate. The only perfect human being to ever walk this earth, whose motives were always pure and actions always deliberate, cried out to God during the opportune time Satan waited for. In the Garden of Gethsemane—yes, another garden—Jesus found himself in a barren, dry, dead place where even his closest friends would not stay awake to pray with him. He was alone. He was worn out. His body was so racked with emotional turmoil that he sweat drops of blood, a medical condition known as hematidrosis. Jesus was about to be betrayed by a close friend named Judas. He knew the cross was coming. It was a valley not filled with just the "shadow" of death. This was a valley worse than the one David was in when he recited Psalm 23. It was the valley of death itself.

On the cross Jesus would quote Psalm 22: "My God, my God, why have you forsaken me?" (v. 1). When a rabbi stood in a synagogue to teach he would begin by reading a passage of Scripture, since people didn't possess scrolls of Scripture at their homes, and his listeners would know, "Oh, okay, this is the passage of Scripture we are going to listen to and discuss today." And since many of those listeners had large portions of Scripture memorized, they would know the full context of the passage as well.

Jesus, crying out on the cross, wasn't only saying he was convinced God was forsaking him; rather, he was also drawing attention to Psalm 22. The onlookers would know it from memory. They would mentally complete the passage:

> My God, my God, why have you forsaken me?
>   Why are you so far from saving me,
>   so far from my cries of anguish?
> My God, I cry out by day, but you do not answer,
>   by night, but I find no rest. . . .
> Do not be far from me,
>   for trouble is near
>   and there is no one to help. . . .
> All the rich of the earth will feast and worship;
>   all who go down to the dust will kneel before him—
>   those who cannot keep themselves alive. (vv. 1–2,
>   11, 29 NIV)

The language of this psalm is striking. God feels so far away. Trouble is near and the enemy is at hand. Circumstance does not line up with God's character. Alone. But not alone. There is a feast. Even those who go down to the very dust of the earth will kneel before him. The situation is not hopeless. Eden is not a desert. Eden is a delight. It is in this garden that spiritually seems like the valley of the shadow of death where the blooming occurs. Who would ever think something good could come from a loving, compassionate individual like Jesus being betrayed, violated, tortured, and murdered?

Those who experience the grace found in Christ alone know exactly what could come from it. Does God still work good from circumstances we would choose to avoid? Romans 8:28 says so. "All things work together for good to those who love God" (MEV). Even when we don't feel it or currently see it this side of heaven.

It was in the wilderness, the barren place, where Jesus had to put whether he truly believed what the Father said to the test. I wonder what it is about the wilderness. Maybe it's there, away from all of the noise, that we are able to identify his voice more clearly. He speaks identity over us. The very thing in your life you desperately want to see triumph in can serve as a clue. To what? To another area in your soul where a lie must be dethroned. Your chalkboard not only contains the lies you've believed but also truths about yourself you have overlooked.

When we walk through—not around but through—the valley of the shadow of death, we don't need to fear evil. Why? We can say with confidence, or more accurately with faith, that *You are with me.* Our valley is simply an amphitheater perfectly designed and conducive to hearing the voice of God. When fear pokes its head up, let it serve as a reminder that God is going to come through for you. In our house, one of the things we will say to ourselves when something unexpected and difficult arises is "It will be fun to watch what God does."

The Song of Your Valley

I once heard a story about groups of mothers in certain African tribes who venture into the wilderness as soon as they discover a woman is expecting a child.[2] Mothers to be, along with a handful of friends, will pray and wait with one another in the barren place until they hear what is known as the song of the child. Each person has their own unique song. They believe every human soul has its own way of expressing its purpose through music. As the women listen, and hear the rhythm of the heart deep within the womb, they begin to sing out loud. The women then return to their village, where they will summon the old and young alike to teach everyone in the tribe the song of the child.

During key life moments, like the child's birth, the village gathers and sings the unique song. As the child grows, is weaned, and begins to start learning, the song is again sung over the child. Emergence into adulthood welcomes yet another time when the song will be heard in the hills surrounding the village as the young adult sits and absorbs the song. And when the soul will pass from this life to the next, what greeted the newborn baby will send the dying one into the hereafter. All of these milestones serve to remind the baby, child, adolescent, young adult, and adult what was spoken over them.

There is one additional time when the village may gather to sing. If at any time the individual begins to wander from the path of wisdom, maybe engaging in taboo behavior or committing a crime against another villager or compromising their identity, the village will gather and sing. Why? Because they believe that what causes someone to step back onto the right path is not punishment but knowing and remembering one's true identity. What was heard in the wilderness long before anything really made sense to the person is what carries him/her through life. Just like David and just like Jesus, their identity dances to the tune of singing.

What Jesus heard in the wilderness carried him through the temptation in the desert and the deep pain in the Garden of Gethsemane. It is in the wilderness, according to the prophet Hosea, where we can encounter God. "I am now going to allure her; I will lead her into the wilderness and speak tenderly to her" (Hosea 2:14 NIV). It is also in the wilderness where the bride encounters her groom in Song of Songs: "Who is this coming up from the wilderness?" (3:6 NIV). In this verse the bridegroom is emerging, and in Song of Songs 8:5 they both are as she leans on her beloved. The bride isn't in the wilderness alone. They both emerge together.

That night I met Jesus I experienced some fairly remarkable things. My body was supernaturally and instantaneously healed. My addiction to substances subsided and vanished. It's almost as if I met myself for the very first time. I went home that night and grabbed a Bible from a cedar box we had in our living room. I stayed up and read through the entire New Testament. Honestly, I am sure my comprehension wasn't very good, as I didn't have a clue what I was reading. My heart, however, told a different story. The more I read, the more I knew something remarkable had happened to me.

The next day I couldn't wait to get home from school and try reading the Bible again. I'd never read it before. The idea of God speaking the world into existence in Genesis 1 was a brand-new concept to me. I figured if God could intervene in my life and love me, regardless of how messed up I was, then speaking things into existence wasn't too hard for him either. Cracking open a hardened heart like mine seemed, to me, to be the greater miracle of the two. Just like the precious African children, I wanted to come into God's presence and hear my song again, sung through Scripture.

I arrived home and checked the mail before going in. Now, if you're reading this and are under thirty, let me just explain something to you. Your parents and grandparents used to receive something called "mail," and it was delivered by a small car, van, jeep, or at times a mail carrier on foot. Mail was a paper-based product placed in an envelope and physically delivered to homes.

(I have to explain for, to some, it's a new concept thanks to technology and globalization.)

I am not sure why I checked the mail that day. I seldom did. It was the providence of God that it happened though. In that metal box was a handwritten letter from that girl who dared to listen in eighth grade when God whispered to her heart. Though she had written it weeks before, she felt compelled to hold on to it. One day, while walking through the shopping mall, she was impressed again in her heart, and she mailed it. It just happened to land in our mailbox the day after I met God. Coincidence? Not at all.

I remember reading page after page of her answers to the questions I used to ask her about God in middle school. Regardless of whether she had previously been indifferent, embarrassed, or simply didn't know the answers, her relationship with God through Jesus Christ now compelled her to respond to my heart's cry three years later. The answers came just in time. I clearly recall thinking, *I am not the only one who knows what God is like.* That letter, written by a young girl who saw a table prepared for a young man in the midst of his valley, was like water to a dry and weary life. For merely one day after meeting God in a profound and personal way, I already realized how hard life could be even with God near. I never doubted God's love for me, but I did question why, after demonstrating his ability to heal and restore and forgive, he didn't intervene sooner or more.

My new relationship with God revealed that, regardless of where I had been, like David, God *was with me.* He was not too embarrassed to be associated with me in my mess. He was not too weak to leave me in the darkness. He was not too busy to hear my heartfelt cry. With so many things in my life as a new

Christian that I wanted to see change, being able to say to God, *For you are with me* brought a peace beyond understanding. God's presence is the treasure worth seeking and finding. Though I wanted God's intervention in so many ways, his presence was enough. Yet even with this reality, the questions still came.

They always do.

Some, rooted in my Bible reading, were things like, "Who is Solomon, and why did he build a temple?" "What is a Pharisee and a Sadducee, and why were they so mean to Jesus?" Others, a bit less theological, were things like, "Why did God save me from that horrific car accident but didn't save my friend from something similar?" I do remember the first time I read Psalm 23. I wondered why God was mentioned in the valley of the shadow of death, because, after all, he must only be near when things are good. Right? It only took a day or so for me to realize how life in God is shrouded in mystery and he rarely explains why. I'm okay with that. So was David.

Some of the answers I was given by well-meaning people seemed void of real life, real emotion, and real love. I didn't need a theological treatise. My heart's cry was beyond the confines of language. My puzzle lid just didn't line up with all of the pieces I found in my heart. I didn't need things to be fixed. I just needed to know I wasn't alone and that God never, ever leaves. I needed to know how God, at just the right time, comes near to us in our wilderness. The purpose? To remind us of who we are and what our destiny is. This is how we enter the wilderness, the valley, with the Spirit leading, and we exit the wilderness and valley full of the power of the Holy Spirit.

When your lid gets switched and you no longer have a true perspective of what is being put together right in front of you, what is at stake is your ability to hear the song of God sung over you. As the bride of Christ, we are not alone in the barren place. He is *God with us.* This is why we don't fear when we walk through the same valley David talked about in Psalm 23. We walk courageously, anchored in who we are and who he is. Why? We have heard him speak over us. Indeed, we heard the song he sang over us (Zeph. 3). Our song is found in the wilderness, and our song is found in him (Prov. 8:6). Let him sing over you, for he has a psalm written about you and for you. But to hear it, you're often required to walk into the shadows, where what lurks is very difficult to see.

EIGHT

Whose Shadow Is It, Anyway?

Shadows serve to remind us of something beyond what we see. When I think of a modern-day story depicting the profundity of what is unseen becoming more real than what we do see, I look no further than Joan Murray.[1]

It was September 1999. The leaves were beginning to change color, and crisp autumn mornings welcomed everyone when a new day dawned. It would be just a few months before the holidays came again. Time with family around the fireplace, everyone's favorite cats in the kitchen, and hopefully a little downtime to recover from another year. But Joan Murray, a forty-seven-year-old bank executive in North Carolina, had something else on her mind. She was about to jump out of an airplane 14,500 feet above ground. This successful businesswoman wasn't nervous. Skydiving was a hobby of hers, and she was quite skilled at it. The art of opening a parachute at the proper time was something she had mastered. There was no question in her mind that she would jump, plummet, and land on her feet yet again.

But Joan was in for more than a surprise on this day. Her life was about to change.

Heading toward the ground at eighty miles per hour and having both her parachute and reserve chute fail to open was *not* something she had ever planned for. I'm sure when she pulled the first chute and nothing happened, after a brief moment of panic she remembered a backup chute was available.

We all breathe a sigh of relief when we are able to plan for that moment or circumstance we never want to experience. What do you do when your plans, no matter how well-thought-out or well-executed they are, don't suffice?

Spiraling through the air at rapid speed prevented Joan's reserve parachute from opening properly. Once it finally did open, a mere seven hundred feet from the ground, it was too late. Joan landed with such a traumatic and powerful force that, upon impact, the right side of her body was shattered. The fillings in her teeth were even knocked loose.

As she lay on the ground, her semiconscious body was racked with pain. I can only imagine the pain and shock she experienced. What flashes through your mind in a moment like that? Do you regret ever adopting skydiving as your hobby? Do you wonder if your family is okay? Do you think about the things you would change in your life if you could do it all over again? Do you mentally and spiritually prepare to step from this life into the next? When the paramedics arrived and raced her to a nearby hospital, the damage to her body was inestimable. She wavered between life and death; every moment she breathed her life was in the balance. She was in a coma for two weeks at the

Carolinas Medical Center in Charlotte, North Carolina. Her body retained fluid as she swelled from her injuries. Her 115-pound body was unrecognizable, but that wasn't the only thing confounding some of the medical professionals. Something else caught their attention.

Where did all the stings and bites on her body come from? There were over two hundred of them.

Ironically, when Joan Murray hit the ground, she landed on top of a massive colony of fire ants. Talk about a bad day! Imagine lying on the ground, wondering whether or not you would even survive, while being stung by fire ants. One after another, the tiny little monsters inflicted pain on the skydiver. Those stings, however, may well have saved her life. Health professionals estimated the ant stings shocked her heart with the perfect amount of electricity to keep her alive just long enough for the paramedics to arrive.

Joan Murray recovered. Six weeks later, after a long journey, she returned home from the hospital. While the healing process was long and painful, in July 2001 she went for her thirty-seventh skydiving jump. This time, just like all of the others but one, she landed perfectly.

When a family goes to the beach with their little one, selecting the perfect place to spread the beach blanket is important. You don't want to be in a vortex of blown sand that will get in your eyes. You want to be close enough to the shore to enjoy the sounds but far enough away to avoid soaking all of your belongings. And no one intentionally sets their blanket on top of a mound covered in fire ants. The very circumstance we would all choose to avoid is the very thing Joan became grateful for. When Joan plummeted to the earth on that horrific day, the small, stinging ants she couldn't see became the bridge to her tomorrow. What was unseen brought back her life.

I am unsure if God is responsible for sending the fire ants that day. There are some things in this life without a divine cause. There are also moments when God does intervene, especially in mysterious ways, and he provides a little assistance to his children. I am not sure why God chooses to intervene in some matters and not others. Theologians create well-versed and intricately rehearsed answers for things like this. I will leave that up to them. I am in no way opposed to sound, orthodox teaching. It is certainly a necessity in our relativistic age. I am, however, always mindful that God chose "the foolish things of the world to shame the wise" (1 Cor. 1:27 NIV) and that God's ways are not our ways (Isa. 55:8). There are moments in our spiritual lives just like the story of Joan Murray. Sometimes what we cannot possibly predict or plan for occurs, and we find ourselves on the other side with a different perspective.

This is one reason why Scripture is pivotal in the life of every believer. God's Word provides a glimpse to what is on the other side of our valley. In essence, it is his *staff*.

Lenses and Mirrors

As a literary work, the Bible is a masterpiece. As a historical document, archaeologists continue to unearth proof that down to the minutia of the page, we can trust what's in it. The story of God reflected in the lives of those we read about offers a different perspective to each one of us. We fine-tune our ability to see what is blind to the naked eye just like the fire ants were invisible to Joan from 14,500 feet above the earth.

Meeting God through Scripture is a commitment no one regrets. God longs to be with you. Scripture is almost like a divine filter through which you can pass every thought, experience, memory, and decision in life to end up at God's best destination for you. I am thankful for how his *staff* comforts me.

The pages of the Book are also like a mirror where you can see yourself for who you truly are. It has less to do with who we are in Christ and more to do with who we are becoming in him. God's Word is a window where we peek into a world much more tangible than ours. Sometimes the comforting assurance of God's love in Scripture makes us very, very uncomfortable. We realize we aren't as put-together as we thought. God comforts us by revealing how our perspective is different from his. In his mercy, he provides a way for us to change our mind and adopt his. When the Holy Spirit communicates with us through Scripture, it isn't to punish; rather, it is to discipline. Scripture becomes his *rod* to provide correction and his *staff* to provide direction. Both are fueled by his unfailing love.

What you must remember is this: God already sees the day when you will stand on the other side of your valley. He has already been there. He prepares a place for you and prepares you for that place. God wants all of your heart, and he will not allow a piece of it to be left behind. So he tenderly and methodically comforts you in your valley. The Bible allows you to see God's work, though it is invisible to the naked eye.

Your Story in Scripture

Several years ago, I was sitting downstairs in our former home in Iowa, minding my own business, when I heard a banging noise coming from upstairs. We had two young daughters, ages four and six, so needless to say I was at least a little bit concerned. Immediately, I made my way upstairs. That's when I found my four-year-old daughter, Dallon, jumping on top of her princess Bible.

Like any good parent would do, I paused for a moment. Standing discreetly at the door of her bedroom, I watched her and marveled at what might be going on in her little brain. After a few minutes of studying her cuteness, I stepped into her room.

"Sweetie, what are you doing?" I asked.

"Oh, I just want to get into the Bible," she said. "So I can be with Jesus." Sometimes what occurs to children is the most raw and honest reflection of what should occur to us. It is possible for the breathtaking reality of God's presence to be our reality, as it was in the narratives and poetry we find in Scripture. Let's take the story of Daniel, for example.

Like he did, we can emphatically embrace the God who draws near. During this season of time, there was a unique relationship between the prosperity of a nation and perception of its deity. For a country to lose a war meant their gods or goddesses were executing judgment on them, or at the least were not interested in their affairs. The Israelites were the only people group who were monotheists, for they worshiped only one God. Not only did they worship only one God but they believed their God was sovereign. We find hints of this orthodox belief all throughout the pages of Hebrew Scripture.

One of the gods of Canaan was Baal. People prayed to Baal for a prosperous crop, believing this god would cause rain to fall on the land. When the psalmist writes of God riding on the clouds and the lightning, it is a reference to the God of the Hebrews sitting higher than Baal. Just one subtlety the poet uses to show Yahweh is highly exalted above all.

What do you do, Daniel, when you are raised in a home and taught your God is sovereign over all other gods, and then, one day, the Babylonian army destroys your city, your leaders, and your temple? The slaughter of the innocents occurs and the God of the Hebrews appears absent. For there to no longer be a nation known as Israel sent a message to the surrounding nations that the God of Daniel was dead. For there to no longer be a temple meant God's presence was gone, and any hope for forgiveness with God was over.

Yahweh had gone missing and didn't prevent the catastrophe, and now those remaining would worship Marduch, the Babylonian god. In a horrific circumstance where God's people were murdered and displaced from their homeland, we read time and again of previous moments in Scripture where God had intervened and preserved them.

Why didn't God prevent it this time?

That question becomes less important when you read the story of Daniel and witness the mysterious fourth man in the fire. Our view of history reveals the presence of God during his perceived absence. The story inspires us, and we think, *Of course God came through for Daniel when he was in the den of lions. God can do anything.*

If Daniel were having coffee with you and describing his valley, knowing what you do from Scripture, you might say, "I'm so sorry this is happening. I understand why you feel the way you do. Remember, God is who he says he is! I'm not asking you to hold on, my friend; I am asking you to buckle up, because the goodness of God and his grace are about to explode in your life in many ways. I know, because I've read the story to the end, Daniel."

For some reason, when we experience something similar in our life, and we have every reason to believe our God is near, we think he is absent. We no longer trust God when our circumstance gives us the slightest reason or inclination not to.

In the prophecy of Malachi, God says he never changes (Mal. 3:6). According to the author of Hebrews, Jesus remains the same yesterday, today, and forever (Heb. 13:8). It is easy to think in our confusion and hurt that God suddenly changed his mind and decided to become a chameleon. All too often we take what we think we know and rationalize our unbelief. At the risk of sounding calloused, although God weeps with us in our pain and dances with us in our jubilation, our self-centeredness surfaces when we think God's character evolves simply because we experience difficulty and tragedy. The human condition is gloriously beautiful and frighteningly fickle. We think God loves everyone else but us and provides breakthrough and comfort for all of his children but us. This is an attitude of the heart that God, in his love, must correct.

Your valley is not the end of the story, however, and you must embrace this by going to his Word. God's story is your story. What you read in Scripture indicates who he is, what he can do, and equally as important, what he will do. Like my daughter Dallon, you don't need to jump up and down on the Bible to try and get in there. Whether you realize it or not, you are in God's story day after day. Your story may not be recorded in Scripture on this side of heaven, but we do know it is recorded somehow and somewhere on the other side.

Revelation 20:12 says, "And I saw the dead, great and small, standing before the throne, and books were opened. Then another book was opened, which is the book of life. And the dead were judged by what was written in the books, according to what they had done." There is a book of life where names of those in Christ are recorded, and they inherit eternal life in God's presence. There are other books opened as well. This text says they record the deeds we do. We know that we are judged not only by what we do but by what we don't do. I submit to you that there is a story written for each one of us by God's divine hand. The choices we make in this life do affect whether or not that story is realized.

Daniel wouldn't have walked into Babylon rejoicing. His family and friends were dead, harmed, or missing. He had every reason to believe God left him. His circumstance certainly didn't line up with the sovereignty he'd heard about. Yet Daniel trusted God and reminds us, "the people that do know their God shall be strong" (Dan. 11:32 KJV). Daniel came to a place where his God was bigger than what he experienced. David came to the same place when reciting Psalm 23. You and I can come to that place too. Sometimes we can be somewhere special and be completely oblivious to it.

Overlooking and Ignoring

I was visiting Spain for the first time. After a busy morning, I sat down with a friend and quite a few strangers for some soup and sandwiches. The soup was cold. When I brought it up, I was informed it was supposed to be. It was gazpacho, a soup fit for the gods, and we also had some of the best ham you can fathom. In Spain, they take their ham seriously. I ate two heaping bowls and enough ham to make a pig farmer in Iowa blush. We walked outside and my friend and host told me I was standing on special ground. It was the very field where Don Quixote tried to change the world. I responded by asking who Don Quixote was. As my friend looked at me in bewilderment, I quickly surmised that I should know who this Don Quixote fellow was. I chose to humble myself and ask.

Known as Alonso Quijano in La Mancha, Spain, this real-life man was portrayed as Don Quixote in the eponymous book by Miguel de Cervantes. It is a story of a self-proclaimed knight and his servant Sancho Panza. Don Quixote goes insane by reading too many stories filled with knights, romance, and chivalry. Consumed with his pretend world, he begins behaving like a knight. He believes voices have summoned him to change the world. So he tries. His lack of rest and insatiable desire for information drove him to believe he was in a story that never truly existed.

There I was, in Spain, standing on the very ground where the real-life Don Quixote supposedly stood. I was standing on literary holy ground, unbeknownst to me, and would've missed it unless someone pointed it out. You too are standing on holy ground, not because of a literary character but because the ground you walk on was paved by God. The bush is burning for you just like it was for Moses. The path that has led you to where you are, according to David, is a righteous path. The same God who was present with Daniel even when he seemed absent is with us all. God's story written in Scripture is our story too, and we must revisit it in the valley.

One of those stories I find myself revisiting over and over again is found in Acts 5. We are told by Dr. Luke, the Gentile physician who wrote the book of Acts, that Peter found himself in the middle of a miraculous display of God's personal affection for the sick. People were brought to the walkways so that Peter's shadow would pass over them. When this happened, Scripture records, they were healed of their illnesses. What an amazing story!

I don't doubt this story for a moment. I wholeheartedly embrace the authenticity of Scripture. In the natural world, God's healing was observed when Peter's shadow passed over the sick. What we see, however, is not all there is. In the unseen world, it wasn't Peter's shadow that healed anybody. It was God's. Let me explain. Psalm 91:1 says, "He who dwells in the shelter of the Most High will abide in the shadow of the Almighty." Peter lived a life in the presence of God and found himself dwelling under God's shadow. We know the whole story, don't we? Peter would agree. It was ultimately God's shadow that healed the sick, for without God's intervention and power, the frail human we call Peter could do nothing by himself.

When we embrace the presence of God in our lives, regardless of what we feel or what circumstance we find ourselves in, we can do much more than jump on top of our Bible and hope it becomes our experience. We can find ourselves in the shade only our heavenly Father can provide. Psalm 23 tells us that death has a shadow and we walk through it. However, don't lose sight that you are under a much larger shadow. It is the shadow of the Almighty. And just like God's shadow partnered with Peter's and saw painful and desperate situations turn around, God's shadow will partner with yours and even death's to watch your valley bloom. The green pasture and the valley of the shadow of death are the same place. Being found in the shadow of God can unearth royalty.

Shadows Are Strong

As a shepherd, David would be familiar with shadows. That word in Psalm 23 for "shadow of death," *tzalamut*, literally translated "deep darkness," serves as a reminder that lurking within the darkness may very well be a predator waiting for an opportune time to pounce on a ewe lamb. Sleeping under the stars and living a nomadic lifestyle isn't for the faint of heart. David was used to the stars. He was used to the shadows. He learned how to see when the light was dim, if present at all, when a break in the path ahead could break the leg of one of his sheep. He killed a lion and a bear as a shepherd. I'm not sure if it was during the daytime or the nighttime, as I've been told lions typically hunt at night or in the early morning hours. What I do know is there were times when a shadow was evidence that danger was near. Regardless, shadows always point to a larger and brighter reality from beyond.

I was in the path of totality when the solar eclipse occurred in 2017. I was scheduled to be in a meeting and, lo and behold, I had the opportunity to put on some glasses and walk outside to see what most people never see. In a small town in Missouri, an estimated one million people were hitting the highways to witness the solar eclipse. The roads were crammed with people. I saw tents along the side of the road. Some people were holding up signs pointing to the apocalypse and the end of the world. It was quite a sight. Those of us in the meeting took our lunch break strategically to go see what all of the hype was about. I have to admit, it was pretty cool seeing the sun "disappear" for a while. It became fairly dark out, but it wasn't pitch black. Do you know why? Even though the sun was hidden, it is so massive that its light still illuminated the earth. What I saw right alongside the solar eclipse was evidence that the very shadow I viewed was proof of something much, much bigger.

Shadows exist because light does. There really isn't such a thing as darkness inasmuch as there is absence of light. One of the descriptors for Jesus is the Light of the World. John tells us that the light shone but the darkness did not understand it. The reason the valley of the shadow of death is filled with shadows is there lies a Light from beyond that shines—regardless of how dark it seems. We do know the enemy is there in the valley. He certainly has a shadow. We also know God is there, for he leads us beside the still waters and comforts us with his rod and staff. We are told that "Heaven, even highest heaven, cannot contain [God]" (2 Chron. 2:6). God is light in whom there is no shadow or turning (James 1:17). He is much larger than our enemy. And although there is no shadow in him, his presence is sure to engulf every other shadow in the way. I don't think the shadow is that of a predator, nor do I think it is that of our enemy. The shadow in the valley is indicative, in my opinion, of the nearness of God even when death itself is close.

For those who seek God, we come out of darkness "into his marvelous light" (1 Pet. 2:9). There, in the light, as we abide in the secret place, we dwell "in the shadow of the Almighty" (Ps. 91:1) and are kept under the "shadow of [his] wings" (17:8). To the modern mind, all of the scary things lurk in the shadows during those tense moments in the movies or novels. We tell spooky stories around the campfires when shadows dance around the flames. But we are commanded to fear God. We are never commanded to fear the valley or our enemy in Scripture. To the God-centered mind, shadows are always a clue that he is close, so close we are engulfed by him. This way of thinking opposes the mind and offends our heart. This is why the Bible comforts us through divine direction and correction. Scripture illuminates all things, even those in deep darkness, to see who is near.

The Old Testament law is considered a "shadow" of Christ (Col. 2:17). Ancient Hebrews believed the anointing of the Spirit extended as far as someone's shadow. Shadows aren't to be feared. This is good news for all of us because Jesus, according to Luke 1:79, came to shine "on those living in darkness and in the shadow of death, to guide our feet into the path of peace" (NIV). If we focus on the shadow of our enemy, we will miss out on the feast prepared for us. It's true.

The great David, chosen by God to be king yet fleeing for his life from the jealous and tyrannical king Saul, would've seen the shadows of Saul's elite soldiers searching for him in the forest. The psalmist would also remember how out of the shadows a lion came to kill one of his precious sheep. If God could deliver David from the lion, surely he could protect David yet again. David had peace that the God who never changes hadn't suddenly and impulsively decided to.

Peace and Circumstance

Peace has a habit of finding us in those places where we finally notice it has been absent. It's an irony, isn't it? Holocaust survivor Elie Wiesel, who at the age of fifteen was deported to a Nazi death camp, said of his experience, "I have not lost faith in God. I have moments of anger and protest. Sometimes I've been closer to him for that reason."[2] Mr. Wiesel's words show us that even in the perceived absence of God during this horrific time in history, God could still be trusted. A holocaust survivor teaches us all that beyond the shadow is something—more accurately, Someone—who is steady.

In our world of changeable comforts, God is unshaken. There is a lot of teaching floating around that God uses difficult seasons to mold us. That is true to some extent, even if God is not the originator of the pain, as I understand Scripture. It is also true, as we've already discussed, that those difficult seasons also reveal who we really are and where God's best is found. I would like to add another piece to the puzzle, assuming our lid doesn't get switched. What if the valley David muses about in Psalm 23 is also an invitation to discover that vast, looming presence lurking behind that little obstruction causing the shadow?

If we look into our cosmos with either the naked eye or the Hubble telescope, the narrative remains constant: we peer back in time. Astrophysicists agree that, because light has a speed, when we look into the sky and take in the light emanating from distant stars, we are looking at what "was." Some stars have burned out yet still shine in our evening sky. Some of the light from distant galaxies seen in observatories is a mere shadow. Our universe is so vast that what we see is actually not.

The peace of God is something our soul is famished for. In my life, like the stars in the sky, sometimes I find comfort in what I think is real simply because it can be experienced. Some of the most profound truths in Scripture are not immediately experienced: they are held closely. God's peace is such.

Attributed to Antoine de Saint-Exupery, author of *The Little Prince*, is this quote: "If you want to build a ship, don't drum up people to collect wood and don't assign them tasks and work, but rather teach them to long for the endless immensity of the sea." The immensity of the sea? Yes, immense with the unknown, shipwrecks, storms, catastrophes, and dangers. It is also immense with discoveries, sunsets and sunrises, memories, and treasures. Fixing our gaze on the shadow is not only a mistake but it is also partnering with something inferior to the truth of God's relevant and powerful Word. We can be destined for victory yet distracted by what we think is there. We must choose to set our eyes on who God says he is. His Word and his heart are inseparable.

As a child, I was introduced to a poem by Max Ehrmann entitled "Desiderata," one line of which is, "Nurture strength of spirit to shield you in sudden misfortune. But do not distress yourself with dark imaginings."[3] I can picture David sitting in the cold Hereth night surrounded by shadows. He chooses not to distract himself with dark imaginings or sabotage his personal victory because he allowed his lid to get switched. He sits in quiet, for he knows if he makes a sound his life may be seized. The still waters flow around him. His soul is being restored at a time when it should wither. He can't see God with his natural eye. And still he has learned and models how, even in deep pain and mystery, we can receive comfort from indisputable spiritual truths.

Like Joan Murray, who found a miracle in the fire ants, David sees God at work with the eyes of his soul. He is not distracted by anything as he audaciously declares *I will fear no evil, for you are with me*. How does David know this to be true? He has received comfort from God's *rod and staff*. Though prone to wander, David kept his heart aligned with who God is and what God does. It is possible to fear no evil, even when the logical response says otherwise.

NINE

Comforted by Engraved Stories

Your rod and your staff, they comfort me.

I
n 2012, Julio Diaz was a thirty-one-year-old social worker from the Bronx with a daily routine.[1] Every night on his way home from work, he got off the New York subway one stop early so that he could eat at his favorite diner around the corner. One night in particular, Julio stepped off the train onto a virtually empty platform, like usual, where he was greeted by something he didn't expect. There, standing on the platform, was a teenage boy with a knife who demanded Julio give him his wallet.

On the one hand, the decision for Julio was easy. Of course he would hand over his wallet. It didn't make sense to risk his life for the sake of some cash. But rather than just simply handing over his wallet, in that moment, Julio decided to do something else too. He offered his coat to the young man.

"If you're going to risk your freedom for just a few dollars, you must really need the money," Julio said to the boy. "Here, go ahead and take my coat too. Otherwise you'll freeze out here." The young man looked at him, stunned.

"In fact," Julio suggested, "why don't you come with me? I'm about to walk down the street and get a bite to eat. I'll buy you dinner." So the young man followed Julio down the street to the diner.

While at dinner, practically every person in the restaurant came by the table to say hi to Julio. The waiters came by. The cooks came out from the kitchen. Even the dishwasher came out to shake hands with Julio and say hello. The young man was shocked.

"Geez, you know everyone in this place! Do you own it or something?"

"No, I just come here a lot."

"But you even said hi to the dishwasher," the young man said to him.

"Yeah," Julio replied. "Didn't anyone ever teach you to treat people with respect, regardless of their position?"

"Of course. I just didn't think anyone actually lived that out."

Julio and the young man finished their dinner, and after the waiter had dropped the bill and cleared their plates, Julio looked right into this young man's eyes. "Look," he told him. "You have my wallet. So if you want to give it back to me, I can treat you to dinner. But if you want to keep it, you're going to have to pay." The young man, without hesitating, handed the wallet back to Julio. He paid for dinner, convinced the young man to trade him the knife for twenty bucks, and then sent the young man back into the night, a changed man. That is the power of embracing peace when your situation gives you a reason not to. If Julio could do it out of sincere decency toward a young man who wanted to rob him, how much more can we do it when we sit under God's shadow in a valley we were destined not to lie down in but to simply walk through?

The voice you listen to the most is where you receive your comfort. David said God's *rod and staff comforted him*. It is convenient, though toxic, to receive a twisted form of comfort from those words spoken and written on your chalkboard. Self-pity only takes your eyes off the One whose grace empowers you and places them on yourself. Quiet loneliness and desperation call out to us and relentlessly pursue us. Their goal? To convince you that, in your situation and only yours, God is not who he says he is.

When you walk through the valley, what comes to your mind? Some remember words spoken over them from a harsh parent or guardian. Some fall headlong into a depressed state as they contrast the physical, sexual, mental, or emotional abuse they suffered as a child or teenager with their current pain. Somehow the two become connected, and an individual will blame him- or herself for occurrences beyond their control. You may think things can't change. You may convince yourself that you're destined for less than what God promised. Do you ever think forgiveness has run out and there is no grace left for you in your valley?

There is still grace for you.

Others find things written on their chalkboard not by the hand of a bully or enemy but by their own hand. How so? Sometimes the choices we make have consequences. I think anyone reading this would agree. A rational person would not blame a judge for revoking their driver's license when he or she operated a vehicle while intoxicated and caused damage or harm. Something more elusive than our choices that plays a lead role in this drama is our thoughts.

David had many toxic things to think about when he recited Psalm 23. In other psalms attributed to David, we catch a glimpse of his humanity. There are times he wanted vengeance on his enemies and other times he blamed God for things God didn't do. I am not here to criticize David. Was he perfect? Not at all. He was, however, a man after God's own heart (Acts 13:22). I can't help but wonder if one of the reasons why this was true is because he learned how to be vulnerable before God in the mysteries.

David didn't ignore what was on his chalkboard. He acknowledged that he was in a valley surrounded by some really scary shadows. And from that place of childlike honesty before God, David learned where to go to receive comfort. The "dark imaginings" from Max Ehrmann's poem are also called "vain imaginations" in Scripture. What we think and choose to dwell on literally shapes who we are. Someone once said we "become what we behold."

Can Butterflies Think?

For nearly three decades, Dr. Caroline Leaf has conducted research on the brain. She has catalogued a massive body of research showing that up to 80 percent of physical, emotional, and mental health issues today could be a direct result of our thought lives. Thoughts are basically electrical impulses, chemicals, and neurons. They look like trees with branches, and as the thoughts grow and become permanent, more branches grow and the connections become stronger.

For every memory you make, Leaf says, you have a corr-esponding emotion attached to it, which is both stored in your brain and as a photocopy in your body's cells.[2] Literally, as a person thinks in his or her heart, "so is he" (Prov. 23:7 KJV). In fact, our thoughts create changes right down to genetic levels, restructuring our cells' makeup. Billions of cells in our body wear out and need to be replaced every day. The lining of the intestines, for example, wears out every seventy-two hours, which means your body is constantly storing memories not only in your brain but in your body. You are a makeup of your environment. What a sobering reality this is. We need a major, miraculous overhaul of our minds if we're ever going to be able to navigate the life Jesus died for us to embrace.

The Hebrew word for "comfort" in Psalm 23:4 is also trans-lated "repent" or "change the mind." The discomfort we feel and experience when we work through our thoughts and emotions to embrace the mind of Christ is actually a form of spiritual comfort. David knew the power of meditating on God's truth. He was committed to a lifestyle of pastoring or stewarding his thoughts and receiving comfort from what God had to say about his situation. A thought seemingly as minuscule as one flap of a butterfly's wing can affect your tomorrow.

In 1960, an MIT meteorologist named Edward Lorenz was busy trying to develop a computer program to simulate and forecast weather conditions.[3] During the experiment, he made an incredible discovery—one that would change the scientific world forever and reveal something God had known all along: something very small can change the course of history.

One day, as Lorenz entered his data from the day before, he was in a hurry, so instead of entering .506127—the number he had used in an earlier trial—he rounded the number to the nearest thousandth, or .506. Lorenz figured the decision would be inconsequential. After all, he estimated the difference was the equivalent of a puff of wind created by a butterfly's wing. He left the lab and went about his business, not thinking anything about it.

When he returned, he found a radical change in the simulated weather conditions. In other words, the difference between the number he'd been entering and the one he'd rounded to—the "butterfly effect"—had dramatically altered the conditions of the weather within the simulator and wreaked havoc in the imaginary world. The real-life impact could literally have been trillions of dollars in damages and countless lives lost due to severe weather. Lorenz concluded that a minor event like the flapping of a butterfly's wing could conceivably alter wind currents enough to change weather conditions a thousand miles away. What a stark reminder of how fragile life is and how stalwart and intimately involved God is as well.

Take a minute to really grasp the gravity of this. One butterfly randomly flying in Alabama can displace lives in Singapore. There is a fine line between science fiction and scientific research. The wind generated by the butterfly—like the breath of a single faith-filled prayer as it leaves your mouth, or the anxious thought within your heart—changes things. The difference might seem small, but it never is. Faith and worry can be the butterfly effect in your life. Slowing down long enough to hear God's whisper in a junior-high hallway can be as well.

Not long after I was married, I read through the prayer journals of my new bride. That same girl who began praying for me in eighth grade and wrote the letter to me about God that came just in time had also devoted herself to prayer for three and a half years. Regularly, between eighth grade and halfway through our junior year in high school, my one-day bride, along with her mom, cried out to God for my salvation. She knew I wasn't making good decisions. She knew my life didn't measure up to God's best for me. Still, she believed that prayer could impact even the hardest of hearts.

I remember reading in one of her journals, timed around three o'clock in the morning, where she wrote "God, I pray Heath will know you." Only eternity will fully reveal the weight of her breath, similar to that of a butterfly's wing, as she opened up her heart and mouth and asked God to reveal himself to me. One of the privileges in my life is the opportunity to stand in front of literally millions of people and communicate. Sometimes I lecture in a university setting and at other times on the stage of a local church. People like you are reading this book right now and, I pray, are impacted by what you read. But none of it would have happened without the prayers of that young girl. She is my lover, my partner in legacy, my closest friend, and a constant reminder of how weighty little things can be. Pay attention to what you think about, for God may very well be in a conversation with you.

When we repent and recognize that the kingdom of God is here, we become sojourners of an unseen reality. We can live in the kingdom while walking this earth. It sounds mystical and unbelievable. And yet it is what he summons us to. We are aliens and strangers in this world. We long for the environment we were created to live in. We were created to live in his presence. It isn't weird; it's normal.

Many would say we have no shortage of things to be afraid of or worried about in our world. When he recited Psalm 23,

David could have easily crafted a list of everything unfair, unjust, and terrifying in his world. But he didn't. Based on Leaf's research—and scriptural truth—when we look through the lens of fear, we see fear, and when we see fear, we experience it. The cycle continues. When we experience fear, we begin to see more fear. We're like the disciples in the boat on the Sea of Galilee before Jesus calms the storm.

Our minds are susceptible to influence, and that influence is so powerful as to deter us from the realities of the kingdom. Attempting to navigate this world or this Christian life without God inhabiting our self-talk is futile. On your way to work in the morning, does your mind wander to what happened yesterday and negatively set up your day? What are you thinking about as you walk through the grocery store? You may have walked into the store full of joy and ready for your weekend, but by the time you leave you don't want to talk to anyone and you're embarrassed of who you are. What happened? Self-talk happened.

Ephesians 4:14 says we need the Holy Spirit, "so that we may no longer be children, tossed to and fro by the waves and carried about by every wind of doctrine, by human cunning, by craftiness in deceitful schemes." The Holy Spirit saves us from inevitable, slow, spiritual death. We need a new way of thinking. And this way of thinking should be anchored in a truth more concrete than even our circumstance.

Comfort from Truth

David anchored his thoughts and emotions in God's rod and staff. This was the source of his comfort. Like Julio Diaz, he saw well beyond the horizon of his current situation. As a shepherd, he intentionally drew on this specific metaphor for reasons our modern mind may not be familiar with. A shepherd's rod and staff were usually one instrument, though at rare times two separate ones. The rod was used to correct sheep or discipline them when they stubbornly wandered away from the flock. The staff represented a much more gentle and even congenial approach to a sheep that had fallen into a ravine or was meandering toward danger. The staff was also used to direct sheep toward water or food. A sheep, even when hungry and thirsty, is hardly capable of fending for itself in the wild.

How humbling it is that we are called sheep and God is our great Shepherd. A shepherd could pull a sheep out of a pit with the staff or defend it from a predator with the rod. During the heat of the day, as the sheep drank water and the shepherd caught a breath, he could lean on the staff to bring relief to his heels and calves from all of the walking.

The Hebrew letter *lamed* is based on the shepherd's staff. Interestingly enough, it looks like one. As a young boy, David would have gone into the forest to select a young tree from which his rod and staff would be carved to fit his own hand. With meticulous attention to detail, a shepherd boy spent time learning how to use the rod like a club to bludgeon anything dangerous when necessary. At times the rod could also be thrown with pinpoint accuracy to fend off an attack. This same instrument was gently laid on sheep to glance through the wool and look for parasites or wounds. It was also used to count the sheep as they wandered back in through the gate.

There is one more element to the rod and staff we have to discuss. Shepherds would carve significant moments into their staff. It served as a living diary or journal. When David killed the lion and the bear, as he mentioned to King Saul that day Goliath was defeated, that would be such a memory to carve in the staff. It is symbolic to think of something carrying a description of God's previous interventions and encounters being the very thing David used to defend and also comfort himself.

We know from Ephesians 6 that the Word of God is to be used when our greatest enemy is unseen. We know from John's writing while on the isle of Patmos that the "testimony of Jesus," literally what we carved into our staff, is "the spirit of prophecy," an indicator that if God did it in the past then God can do it again (Rev. 19:10). The rod and staff David spoke of is synonymous with how God comforted him. The *Midrash* refers to the Torah as God's rod and staff. Scripture is something the Holy Spirit uses to comfort us.

David learned to steward his own soul during the difficult times. He could have said to himself, *See, even your own dad didn't think you were the one the prophet would choose to be king. He didn't even invite you to the house that day Samuel showed up. If your father doesn't believe in you, then no one can help you.* He could have mused, *I am nothing and always will be*, as many rabbis speculate David was seen by his family as the product of an affair. *People sneer at me all day long. My reputation is never going to be rebuilt. Maybe I should just give up and give in. I would be better off dead anyway.* If he did think or feel any of these things, he didn't stay there.

He learned to pay attention to his self-talk, for indeed it is prophetic and formative. He watched his heart closely to make sure God's perceived absence did not lure him away from the peace only God could provide. When you are in the valley of the shadow of death, the worst thing you can do is ignore your feelings—or, equally, believe every feeling. Our emotions are not bad. God has emotions. For example, have you ever wondered why Jesus wept when he learned Lazarus died? After all, Jesus was going to raise him from the dead. Why would Jesus stand outside of a tomb and weep right before he resurrected someone? It seems trivial to us, but it demonstrates how we can worship God with all of our emotions, even when they seem out of place. Likewise, in all of our honest assessment of how we feel and what we think, let's not get stuck there.

Like David, we take Scripture in our hands and we let God's rod and staff comfort us. Like David, we think about those times God came through for us before. We think about the fact that without God, we wouldn't even be alive. We think about the reality that the same God who knows all three hundred thousand species of beetle also knows our name. We embrace how God, despite knowing every juicy piece of gossip about us, chooses not to destroy our name; instead, God gives us a new name and calls us sons and daughters.

Do you feel like there isn't anything on your rod and staff to comfort yourself with? Think again. One of the reasons we doubt God's presence in our own shadowy valley is we ignore all of the other valleys we've traversed with God and come through in the past. Scripture is described as a light for our path (Ps. 119:105). Why? Often, our life in God requires us to walk in mystery, where we feel like we don't know where we are or where we are going. He illuminates our path. But he doesn't light up the horizon for miles to come. He reveals just enough for us to take the next step. There is a lot written on God's rod and staff pertaining to you. It is God's *rod and staff*.

Remember in Matthew 4, when Jesus was in one of his valleys? He used God's rod and staff to comfort himself, just like

163

David did. Jesus said repeatedly, "It is written." It is just like the African mothers who sing over the unborn children in the wilderness. They revisit what they know to be true about each child. What we believe about our God, our situation, and our very self is our source of comfort or discomfort. We each hold a rod and staff. What if the truth you cling to is inaccurate, twisted, incomplete, or just plain wrong? I know, I know. We live in an age where being "right" seems to be more relative than ever. We aren't talking about politics or contemporary issues right now. We are talking about whether or not your lid, the very thing you are using to build your puzzle, is wrong. We are talking about your focus being on the words written on your chalkboard, yet you—or me, or all of us—overlook the most important and provocative ones that rewrite or even erase the rest.

We all hold a rod and staff we use to comfort ourselves. Some use food and self-medicate with gluttony. Others use opioids or other substances. How do you comfort yourself? Becoming the loudest and meanest in the argument might be your strategy. I've done that. Or avoiding people out of embarrassment, maybe. I have done that too.

When we find ourselves in the valley, our rod and staff can come in the form of shutting down, pornography, anger, depression, or self-loathing, or we may push away the very ones who are willing to sit with us in our mess. If we receive comfort from any rod and staff other than God's, our finite perspective will sabotage our ability to deepen our soul and walk in God's presence even when he seems absent. We end up not seeing the miracle in our mystery. Even when all of the odds are stacked in your favor, if you believe a lie about your situation, you become enslaved by it.

I remember like it was yesterday when I realized how one thought can ruin a life—and even more so, an entire empire.

Empires Fall with Thoughts

The first time I traveled to Guatemala, I was awestruck by the volcanoes, the coffee, and the people. We ventured into a remote area where, away from the tourists, we were able to engage in conversation with a culture much more ancient than I could ever imagine. I found myself talking with an indigenous Guatemalan man on the side of a volcano. In his hand he held a staff or walking stick of some sort. That's pretty ironic, now that I think about it. His goal was to preserve his culture and avoid any taint from the western world. I quickly realized that, as a foreigner, my perspective paled in comparison with what the gentleman thought about his life and culture. I was intrigued when he brought up someone you may remember from history class: Pedro de Alvarado. Alvarado was one of the lieutenants in Hernan Cortes's army and a veteran of the Spanish conquest of Mexico in the early sixteenth century. I had to do some further research.[4]

Guatemala was not inhabited by the mighty Aztec Empire of Mexico or the technologically advanced Incas of Peru. When Alvarado ventured toward the beautiful land I found myself in, he and his less than five hundred Spaniards and Mexican allies found the remnants of something unexpected: the Mayans. The Mayan Empire, which peaked around AD 800, stretched from southern Mexico to Belize and what we now call Honduras. A vast empire built on trading, philosophy, astrology, and architecture had been reduced by the sixteenth century to small conglomerations of a strong warrior people who fought fiercely to preserve their way of seeing the world and lifestyle. The K'iche and Kaqchiquel in central Guatemala were some of the strongest Mayan settlements remaining.

I was struck by the fact that, though the Spaniards had some superiority with their military training and weaponry, they would not have been used to the nooks and crannies of the topography or accustomed to the land at all. The Mayans could easily have ambushed the Spaniards and overwhelmed them with guerrilla-style warfare. The native Guatemalans were stricken by diseases similar to the smallpox breakout that took many of the Incans. The Spaniards, however, were also disease-ridden and at a loss for how to squelch the Mayan passion to survive. We know this from some recently translated letters from Alvarado to Cortes, with additional accounts from one of his cousins, his brother Jorge, and Bernal Díaz and Bartolomé de Las Casas. But in the end, the Spaniards used rivalry between indigenous tribes to manipulate them and bring down a community much larger in number and more familiar with the terrain.

While we can speculate all day long and discuss many of the reasons why this rivalry occurred, the indigenous Guatemalan I met said something that intrigued me. He referenced a vision an Aztec astrologer had centuries before that played a key role in the defeat of a people who, had they united, should have easily defeated the Spaniards.

Also, why would any Mexicans, who personally knew what the Spaniards did to their land and Aztec ancestors, agree to assist the Spaniards with a similar conquest in Guatemala? I decided to do some research in a quest to verify what the Guatemalan man with the staff said to me.

Some of the Mexicans who partnered with the Spaniards to defeat the Mayan settlements believed something spiritual was taking place as the Spaniards enslaved the people, stole their gold, pillaged the storehouses, and destroyed families. They had their lid switched. Some said it was an omen, others a prophecy—and you might think it was too much food before bedtime.

An Aztec astrologer believed something about their god that caused them to be a casualty of their own misunderstanding. Toltec legends mention a light-skinned, bearded man who visited the Indians. This man, known to be a priest-king, said he would return to render judgment. The second coming of this priest-king, Quetzalcoatl, would occur when he came from the east, riding a white demon and accompanied by prophetic signs. After a famine, an earthquake, and the appearance of a comet, some began to wonder if this "omen" was true.

Others had similar experiences. A king named Moctezuma had a vision-like experience where he said a bird's crest revealed to him "fire sticks." The king's sister supposedly had a vision of great ships from a far land with men wearing helmets, holding banners, and having "fire sticks." When the Spaniards arrived, contact with some of these Indians began. Cortes appeared before the great Aztec king Moctezuma II. The king was terrified that the gods had come back to render judgment. With an army carrying fire sticks (guns) and riding demons (horses), this pale, bearded "priest-king," outnumbered 1000 to 1, easily defeated the Aztecs. The people were enslaved, women were raped, gold was stripped from the land, and disease destroyed the vast empire.

So, why would Aztec descendants help less than five hundred Spaniards do the same to the Mayans in Guatemala? Though some speculation and inference is required, we do know this:

the Spaniards never would have made it to Guatemala if the Aztecs in Mexico didn't believe the gods had been judging them when the Spaniards came. Whether you believe the prophecies or omens is no consequence to me. Frankly, I'm not really sure what to do with this information. What I do know is it is well-documented in history that what a king believed about his god caused him to reduce his god to his circumstance.

As a child of the one true God, when you reduce God to your circumstance, you can believe anything and it will enslave you. When you do not allow your circumstance to dictate who God is and you choose to keep walking rather than lying down in your valley, you do exactly what David did. No, it doesn't mean you deny reality and pretend everything is okay. It means you acknowledge you are in a valley, like David did, but you continue to walk and climb and even crawl if you have to in order to get through it. Your strength doesn't just come from how you feel: it comes from who God is. He is there. He is strong. He weeps when you weep. He carries you when you fall. He breathes for you when you don't even have enough strength to go on.

When you are baptized in mystery and feel like you are drowning, God can and does come close. The very shadow you see is proof that well beyond you is Someone much larger who casts a light in your direction. David did not allow his circumstance to be the final narrative he believed. Fortunately, David embraced the comfort that only comes from God's *rod and staff.* Just like a shepherd uses his rod and staff to guide sheep to fresh water and lush pasture, your heavenly Father uses his rod and staff to lead you to a feast as well. And, according to David in Psalm 23, God invites your enemies to watch.

TEN

The Table Your Enemy Can't Feast At

*You prepare a table for me
in the presence of my enemies.*

No one places a precious baby right beside a loud, boisterous, and potentially harmful dog—unless you're Irena Sendler. As World War II began closing down, by 1945 two out of every three European Jews had been killed by the Nazis. Of the six million Jews who were murdered, 1.2 million were children. Of this horrific time in history, holocaust survivor Elie Wiesel wrote, "In those times there was darkness everywhere. In heaven and on earth, all the gates of compassion seemed to have been closed."[1] But Irena Sendler left her gates open. May she never become company with the forgotten ones.[2]

Irena grew up watching her father, a doctor, care for his patients, many of whom were also poor Jews. In adulthood, she became a senior administrator in the health profession in Poland. Appalled at the malevolence against the Jews after the Nazis invaded Poland, Irena became one of the first volunteers to join the Zegota, the Council for Aid to Jews organized by an underground movement, to save Jewish children. As the Nazis scoured the Warsaw ghetto for more and more people, Irena smuggled Jewish children out and worked diligently for them to be adopted by non-Jewish families. How many? She rescued 2,500 children. Their names were changed as they were given to new families. Their original identities were kept in records stored in jars that were buried across the street from the Nazi barracks. There, in the dirt underneath an apple tree, Irena made provision for those children to one day discover their heritage—if, indeed, they ever made it back.

Irena needed a special pass to legally enter the ghetto. Her work with the Epidemic Control Department enabled this to happen. With tears and persuasion, Irena and Jewish families struggled to reach the inevitable conclusion: the families must allow Irena, a complete stranger, to take their children away from them and smuggle them out of the ghetto. The parents would never see their children again.

Children were smuggled out in sacks, coffins, or toolboxes. When the children were leaving their parents, Irena recalled how the moms and dads asked her to guarantee that the children would live. Irena would simply reply that she could only guarantee that if they stayed they would die. The screams of the children being ripped from the arms of the only love they knew tormented Irena in her sleep for years to come, she said.

The children couldn't possibly understand the danger they were in, and their cries made them susceptible to discovery by the Nazis. How do you tell young children to calm down when they have been ripped from their homes in the night? Irena would bring a dog with a vicious bark with her, and at checkpoints its loud barking would drown out the children's cries and fend off Nazi inspections. Who takes little children away from their loving home and places them in a dark vehicle with a vicious and noisy dog? Irena did—when it meant carrying those children away from the Nazis toward a better life.

In the presence of their enemies, the Jewish children found blessing because of the loving sacrifice and presence of Irena Sendler. The valley for 2,500 precious and beautiful sons and daughters was in bloom whether they understood it or not. Eventually, Irena was discovered by the Nazis and faced arrest and torture. She was imprisoned and sentenced to death, but Irena was saved at the midnight hour and was able to escape. She was hunted and chased by the Nazis, but she survived. And when the war had ended, she dug up the jars and contacted as many of the children as she could find and tried to reunite them with their families. While many of the families were no longer alive because of the monstrosities of the concentration camps, some were reunited with their children—who discovered something about their identity on the very ground they would never have chosen to walk through.

David learned a similar lesson when he recited Psalm 23. The very ground we choose not to venture toward, the valley of the shadow of death, has a piece of our identity and a piece of God's identity buried there. What is that piece? We are sons and daughters of the King of kings, and we have been invited to sit at God's table and feast. I think of this imagery when I reflect on the children who receive food from Feed One.

They are surrounded by extreme poverty, malnourishment, disease, and death. The compassionate generosity of others who give, volunteer, pray, and serve reveals how accessible thankfulness is. In Nicaragua, their faces light up when they can eat. In Sri Lanka, they laugh and tease one another over a bowl of food. In the Philippines, they are present in the moment while eating and do not focus on the many challenges around them. These forgotten and abandoned ones feel loved, noticed, and like royalty when someone dares to prepare a physical table for them in the presence of their enemies: injustice, poverty, corrupt capitalism, human trafficking, and the worst of all, feeling unloved. Similarly, God prepares his table, just like Irena did, in the presence of many enemies in your life.

An Unlikely Invitation

Rabbinical tradition and commentaries mention how dilapidated David's health was during this time in the Hereth forest. He was starving to death. The one who delivered food to his brothers during Goliath's taunts had no one to bring him food during a much more difficult battle. No one was attending to David's needs. There was no hot coffee to keep him warm during the cool evening. He couldn't forage or hunt, as it was too dangerous. King Saul's elite soldiers were searching for David and they were well fed. But in the presence of David's enemies, God prepared a table. What did David feast on? He feasted on God's presence. When our emotional, physical, and social circumstances do not provide the comfort and sustenance we need to survive, there is a place of feasting for the human soul before God.

The Jewish culture in the first century understood this ability to feast at the Lord's table. Jewish sages, whose views are recorded in the Mishnah, described and prescribed topics from the Torah to sing, discuss, recite, and explain at meals. Both social and spiritual formation occurred over feasting. Often, someone would observe the meal and its verbal/nonverbal communicative moments and insert key phrases when appropriate. Why? The purpose was to create a metaphor or interpretation of what was taking place. A great example of this is the Passover meal and/ or the Seder. When a spiritual truth was to be reinforced, often it occurred over food. Now we understand how important it was for Jesus to address his betrayal by Judas during an evening meal with the disciples.

David, knowing the significance of conversation over mealtime, chose to reference a Jewish custom he would've been familiar with as well. He discussed it with God personally, for the language he used in the valley, at the table of the Lord, is in first person. *You prepare a table before me; you anoint my head with oil.* David understood the metaphor his circumstance had become.

I just have to stop and address the obvious for a moment. I can understand inviting a few angels to the party. But why would a loving God invite our enemy?

God prepares a party, a table to feast at, in the presence of the very memories and experiences we try to forget. Those circumstances where our greatest pain, regret, disappointment, and doubt exist are placed at the top of the guest list when God writes the invitations. If anyone knows how to throw a party, God does. Why would God do this?

Grateful under the Stars

Well, there are about a dozen reasons I can think of right now, and I am sure there are thousands of others we will never fully understand this side of eternity. Perhaps one reason is that there, in the presence of our enemies, God's love and faithfulness are magnified even more. God is who he says he is. It is in the presence of something we would never willfully choose to celebrate that God comes closer, and we catch another glimpse of who he is. We experience yet another reason why we are to be so thankful and grateful solely for who God is.

You may feel like there is nothing to be grateful for. Maybe your situation is so draining, so hopeless, you don't see how God could or should even be honored. You look at your past and see so many opportunities where God could have intervened but only left you disappointed yet again. Some say hindsight is 20/20. Hindsight, however, is only as clear as your understanding of your experience. Our greatest enemies to being grateful are not intellectual; rather, they are from the heart. Scripture does not say "as [a man] thinketh in his *brain*, so is he." No, Scripture tells us "as [a man] thinketh in his *heart*, so is he" (Prov. 23:7 KJV, emphasis added). We think with our heart. God's perspective is ultimately the truth we embrace. Everything else is mere commentary. The enemy of ungratefulness must bow its knee before God.

The phrase "in the presence" can mean "opposite or far off." "Of my enemies" can mean "adversary, enemy, vexation." Often what we consider to be an all-out assault on our character, our dreams, or our world is actually an invitation by God to feast. When we wander into our valley, we have a choice: we can either become seduced and distracted by the very presence of our enemy or we can turn our back on whatever seeks to diminish the majesty and love of God in our lives. God is the guest of honor at the feast in the valley. It is *for his name's sake*, according to the psalm. His presence is the feast.

Jesus was in a similar state in Matthew 4. Forty days of fasting left his body weak and frail. He was hungry and, having waited for an opportune time, the enemy came to him. Jesus was led by the Spirit into the desert, and after refusing to be distracted by his enemy, Scripture says he left it full of the Holy Spirit. He went in hungry and weak and left full. He was thankful for what he had when he could have become jaded by what he lacked. He feasted on God's presence amid a circumstance that could have destroyed him. At another time, in the Garden of Gethsemane, Jesus was in another circumstance where he was weak and vulnerable. The enemy came again after entering Judas Iscariot. The holiest of all people to have ever walked the earth asked his Father three times to make the cup pass from him, and it did not. Did Jesus doubt God's love? Did he give up and give in? No. He remained thankful and did not allow his circumstance to get in the way of who God is. Sometimes things just get in the way.

Ali and I have two beautiful daughters, and both of them teach us a lot about what it means to be in love with Jesus. Several years ago, I was serving at a summer youth camp. Due to my responsibilities, the busyness with campers and logistics all week, I was lacking one-on-one time with my family members. So one night, around midnight, I took our daughter Leighton out on a golf cart to look at the stars. We drove the cart out onto a big field, into the dark, and straight to what we called "the bump," a raised piece of land I used to drive over really fast to make our stomachs drop. She always thought that was the coolest thing in the world.

Anyway, we drove out to the top of the bump and just sat still, waiting to see a shooting star or a satellite or something I could point out to my awestruck daughter. We just sat there together, staring at the beauty above our heads. That's when Leighton said something I'll never forget. She said, "Daddy, don't you wish we could take away all the stars so we could see Jesus again?"

It's funny the way kids' brains work. Leighton didn't even know exactly what she was saying that day, and yet her words could not have been any truer. So often the things in our lives that are the most magnificent, the shiniest, the brightest—even the clearest reflections of God's sovereignty and grace in our lives—can get in the way of us seeing Jesus. Some of us have heard so many sermons that we overlook the truth God is revealing. Others have been to so many classrooms, conferences, or counseling sessions that we know just the right answer to almost every provocative and mysterious question—and it still just isn't enough. There are a lot of good things that get in the way sometimes. To Leighton, behind the sky was a God who sees. That's a good truth for us all to embrace.

When we learn to come before God and simply be, even when he seems far off and we are surrounded by so many other things, we become stronger. One of the enemies gathering before us in our valley is named *Ungrateful*. There is something inside us all that knows trying to avoid pain and suffering in order to become healthy and whole is foolishness. Those I've known with cancer never celebrated the news of another round of chemotherapy, yet they endured and fought hard, for they saw hope on the other side. When dealing with emotional and spiritual pain, a subtle nuance exists. We know we need to deal with it and feel inauthentic when we celebrate anything else. We tend to think, *I need*

to get through this before I experience any sort of joy or gratefulness.
But being thankful for the many mercies of God in our life, while
going through the difficulties, isn't fake. It is a sign of health.

It is not trite to thank God for the air you breathe today. No,
there is a freedom that comes when you can see him at work in
your trial. When you take a little longer to stare at your child
today, even if it's through teary eyes, you overcome more. When
you celebrate communion with saltine crackers and orange juice
because it's all you have, you remember Jesus in the middle of
the valley. Giving to meet someone else's need, when you have
so many needs yourself, isn't ignoring your financial hardship. It
is seeing the table and choosing to sit down even in the midst
of things that seek your harm.

David said God prepared a table for him *in the presence of
his enemies.* This is why David could say with confidence that
surely goodness and mercy would follow him. David knew how
to lay down in the green pasture while simultaneously walking
through the barren place. Because Jesus learned to feast in the
desert in Matthew 4, he was able to believe God for another
feast in another desert in John 6. Like David saw a reason to
feast, Jesus also saw a feast, even when his closest friends saw no
sustenance within miles. As we will see, a grateful and thankful
heart in the desolate place paved the way for a mystery to turn
into a miracle. It was in the desert where Jesus threw one of his
biggest parties with a child.

Giving Thanks in the Deserted Place

All four Gospel records (Matt. 14:13–21; Mark 6:30–44; Luke
9:10–17; John 6:1–13) share the famous story of Jesus feeding

the five thousand. Only this miracle and the resurrection are mentioned in all four Gospels. When something is mentioned four times in the Bible, it is more crucial than you can fathom.

Jesus crossed the Sea of Galilee with some friends, a four-mile journey by boat, and Mark 6:33 tells us a crowd arrived at the other side of the lake before Jesus did. The distance the crowd traveled on foot would have been around ten miles. We catch a glimpse of thousands of people running around the lake, desperate to be in proximity to Jesus again. What could cause so many people to run that far, that fast, just to get back to Jesus?

If that crowd is like every other crowd, there were people there who were bullied and ridiculed and who found the encouraging words of Jesus life-giving. Some who had been manipulated experienced the authenticity of Jesus and wanted to be with him again. Some who had cried out to God over the years were taken by how accessible and approachable he was. Those haunted by their choices or the choices of others saw no judgment in his eyes. There was something about Jesus that made them run and run and run just to be close to him one more time.

Mark and Matthew describe the location of the miracle by referring to it as a "desert place," while also noting it was colored with green. John 6:10 refers to the place as having "much grass." Luke 9:10 refers to Jesus going into a "desert place belonging to the city called Bethsaida" (KJV). This stands out to me since Bethsaida (modern el-Araj), a first-century fishing village, is in a fertile valley laden with streams and aqueducts. This "desert place" is very different than the desert we would think of today. The description by Mark and Matthew refers to the circumstance, not simply the landscape.

It is in this place, a valley described as both a desert and a green place, where Jesus performs an amazing miracle. A young child places five barley loaves (the bread of the poor) and two small fish before Jesus. John 6:2 and 6:5 use the word *great* to describe the multitude of people, while the fish are *small* (NIV). It is a play on words to show how much the circumstance Jesus found himself in didn't line up with what God could do. What was his response? He found himself in a valley and a green pasture simultaneously, just like David did in Psalm 23. Jesus was in a valley about to bloom.

He took the food, gave thanks, and then began distribution. Jesus was surrounded by hungry, poor people. The mystery turned into a miracle after Jesus gave thanks. Thousands of people were fed in this moment. To showcase this truth further, John 6:23 records that Jesus and his disciples returned to the place where Jesus "had given thanks." It does not say "They returned to the place where Jesus multiplied the bread and the fish." The place is also not referred to as the place "where Jesus fed the multitudes." It is the place where Jesus gave thanks.

Giving thanks in a circumstance diametrically opposed to the Father's goodness is much more miraculous than multiplying bread and fish. That is what's worth remembering, first and foremost. God prepared a table for thousands of poor people, in the presence of poverty, injustice, torment, sickness, suffering, oppression, and persecution. Each one, with their enemy close by or, even more so, within, feasted at a table God prepared for them in a valley. Just like David.

Everybody needs a table to feast at with God. For me, it is literally just that. My favorite piece of furniture in our house is our dining room table. We waited and saved our money to make sure our purchase would stand the test of time. It is heavy, intricately carved, wooden, and just right. One of my dreams is to sit at our table with my children, grandchildren, and great-grandchildren and share a meal together. I plan on having a wide array of cheesy dad jokes to share. I also plan on glancing frequently at all of the beautiful faces around our table as I see with my own eyes proof of the family legacy we are believing God for and working diligently toward.

At this time in our life, there are four of us. Often, as our girls are growing up and becoming increasingly mobile, I cherish our meals together. Sometimes we talk the entire time, and other meals have more silence than words. Being together is a treat for us all, and we make meals a significant time to catch up, talk about God, bring each other up to speed on work and/or school, or, if I have one handy, share a cheesy dad joke.

I often catch a glimpse of Ali in the early morning hours, sitting alone at our table. It is one of my favorite memories and one our daughters mention regularly as well. There she is, sitting with her almond milk latte and stacks of various Bibles, discovering yet another amazing promise and insight she will share with us from her feast with God at our table.

Recently, Ali shared a story with me that depicts how gentle God is with us in our vulnerable state while simultaneously remaining vigilant as our protector.

God Surrounds Us

The African elephant is the largest land mammal on the face of the planet. Their social structure is uniquely tight, especially among the females. When a baby elephant is born, it comes into the world with a relatively small number of survival skills and is immediately dependent on the protection and provision of the herd. Born almost entirely blind, the young animal is often unaware of the dangers lurking so near. Predators gather around to watch for an opportune time to ambush the baby. But when danger is near, the vulnerable elephant is surrounded by the rest of the herd. The predator cannot get through the impenetrable wall of safety, and the daunting sound of the herd's stomping feet is certain to drive away any overly confident killer.

Through the eyes of the infant, danger lurks but is often undetected. Through the eyes of the herd, danger draws near and an urgent appeal for unity is made. The herd comes together to protect the vulnerable. I wonder what the enemy or predator sees. At first glance, I'm sure it believes the baby elephant will be an easy target. To its surprise, however, I can just imagine how disappointment settles in when it discovers the meal it thought was just for it is untouchable.

I can imagine the enemy of our soul feeling the same way. There he is, that enemy who desires nothing more than to discourage and wound us, coming around the corner in the valley. The barren landscape spells sure victory for our enemy. After all, there's no way he believes you are capable of remaining faithful and committed when things are difficult. The same one who tried to incite God to turn his back on Job (Job 2:1–10) is the same one who thinks you only serve God when it is convenient. Exhausted and tired, your face says it all. The enemy studies you closely. He knows you just need to get a break in life. He knows you are frustrated from a prayer life that is reactionary rather than responsive. If only you could catch your spiritual breath then maybe you could finish the long trek out of the valley of the shadow of death.

The enemy comes around the corner and sees you in your helpless state. He thinks he has you. He knows you don't see all there is around you, just like the baby elephant. He sees the table spread in the valley and arrogantly thinks it is provision for him. The feast about to take place is unstoppable, and you are going down. That's what he thinks. But he's wrong.

As he comes around the corner in the valley, imagine how surprised he is when you are now surrounded by protection. Like that herd of elephants, an impenetrable wall now surrounds you. You are untouchable. How can I say that? You can be pressed down but not crushed. You can be persecuted but not abandoned. You can be struck down but never destroyed (2 Cor. 4:7–11). What the enemy thought was a feast for his own selfish gain is his defeat. What you thought was a spiritual attack is God's invitation to come feast at his table in the valley.

Rest assured: you are surrounded and protected when you feel most isolated and under siege. Feel the liberty to take your eyes off of the enemy, for he isn't worth your attention. Fix your gaze on the table God has prepared just for you.

You're Not the Only One

Steeped in the occult, substance abuse, and a host of other lies, I came face-to-face with God's ability to take a hopeless life and soul and rescue it. I had firsthand knowledge that God could supernaturally heal a body racked with illness. It had happened to me. I knew God was not ashamed to step into my mess and hear my cries for forgiveness time and again, because grace seemed so impossible. The guilt I felt for things I did, relationships I violated, and promises I ignored were overshadowed by his love for me. With the truly countless miracles I'd witnessed in less than twenty-four hours of knowing God personally through Jesus Christ, I realized how often circumstances in my life would not line up with what I knew to be true about God. I wondered, *If God can heal, why did my friend have to die of leukemia?* Or, *If God can restore, why do the memories from my childhood still haunt me, and why do I find it so difficult to be close to anyone?*

There are people in church this week who think, during a worship song, of a memory that makes them feel dirty and ashamed. Rather than choosing to thank God for his mercy, maybe they harden their hearts and choose not to be vulnerable before God again. After all, he's probably shocked they are at church to begin with. Right? Well, that's what the enemy says to get our eyes off of the table prepared just for us by God.

You may feel like your problems go increasingly unsolved while everyone else is making progress. Or you look around at everyone in the coffee shop; they are laughing and seem like they have a life full of friends and happy memories. You sit there, alone yet again, wondering if you will ever have a true friend. Do you dread the holiday coming up because it serves as just another reminder of how dysfunctional things are? Do you lack the energy to even dare to think of what your future could look like in God?

It didn't take long for you to realize how people you confide in can turn their backs on you and humiliate you. You were surprised to find out how hypocritical some church people can be, and how controlling and manipulative some of those closest to you are. You became a Christian because you dared to believe Jesus is who he says he is. He forgave you and embraced you. He summoned you into the abundant life. Within a short amount of time, however, you, along with the rest of us, realized how unpredictable life can be and how aloof God can feel at times. It isn't God's fault. You know he is as good as Scripture says. Your circumstance and the voice of reason seem louder than his still small voice. Where is his presence, and why does God seem so absent? Why do so many prayers seem to go unnoticed?

It is a mystery; no, it is a *miracle.* The first truth I learned the night I met Jesus Christ was that he can forgive and restore when we humbly come. The second truth I learned, within twenty-four hours of having my breath taken away by God's grace, is that I must learn to trust God even when my situation gives me logical reason not to. The presence of my enemy does not nullify the reality of God's ever-present table. Irena Sendler prepared a table for thousands of children who saw the miraculous take place in the midst of the holocaust. I have seen hungry children dare to smile again, in the middle of complex national, social, and family circumstances, over a bowl of food. With God we can dare to stand confidently in our valley and green pasture, for, after all, they are the same place. We choose to give thanks when what we have seems like it isn't enough. Thanksgiving is fueled by who God is and not just what we do or do not have. I must—you must—choose to pull up the seat reserved just for you and gently unfold the napkin and drape it across your lap. It is time to feast in God's presence.

I couldn't care less if the enemy watches.

ELEVEN

A Realm of Intimacy

Surely goodness and mercy shall follow me
all the days of my life.

Young Hattie May Wiatt was from humble circumstances, innocent, some say naïve, and altogether the least likely candidate for a miracle. But Hattie May's choices and deep belief in God's grace can inspire us to embrace a God who is wondrously near and who uses our thankfulness to perform miracles.[1]

During a time when hot food and clean clothes were a rare commodity, she traversed the roads of Pennsylvania. She'd heard something about Jesus. We aren't quite sure what, but whatever it was, it motivated her to walk by herself to a church one Sunday. In these days this church in Philadelphia was growing, and the peculiar message of love behind the name of Jesus Christ provoked long lines to form of children seeking to attend a Sunday school class. Hattie was one of them, interested in hearing more about this Jesus of Nazareth. I wonder what she heard to make her so interested.

She waited in line to get into the classroom. Some accounts say the classroom filled up, and Hattie May was turned away along with many other children. I've read other accounts that say chairs were still left in the classroom, but because of her unkempt appearance, she was turned away. Her clothes were soiled, torn, and tattered, unlike the clothes of those who "belonged" at such a religious institution like this one. Regardless, all accounts agree on her response. Hattie May, disappointed at her inability to get into the class with the other children, sat on the side of the road and cried—alone, disappointed, and longing for a change to come. Just like David. Have you ever been there?

Are you longing deep within for that one thing to change or that one moment to come? You put your hope in God with the desire that he will come and prove to you he is indeed good, indeed listening, and indeed capable of meeting your heart's desire.

Where was God when this little girl prayed for a chance to go and hear more about Jesus? Well, he stopped beside her and knelt down.

As she sat, crying, a gentleman noticed her. I imagine she would've been similar to that young girl in second grade who had everyone walk up to the chalkboard and painted her green pasture with shadowy words. But this time, in that moment of sorrow, someone drew near. I imagine the initial conversation going something like this:

"What is the matter, sweetie?" I can hear his deep voice ask her as he crouched down to her level. Deep enough to soothe

186

but not to scare. She didn't run away. Something made her feel safe enough to respond.

"There isn't any more room left in the classroom. I wanted to hear about Jesus and I can't."

"Well, I'm sure we can find you a seat. Come, take my hand, and let's see what we can do."

He took her by the hand, walked into the classroom, and found a spot for her. He also sat with her for most of the class. This gentleman, who happened to be the pastor of the church, might have leaned over to her and said something like, "I must go now, sweetie. You stay right here. I have some things to attend to, but I will see you again next week. Okay?"

They struck up quite the friendship, the pastor and young Hattie May. They said hello to one another and often walked down the road together. A young girl, so desperate and so broken that all she wanted was a chance to hear something hopeful about God, had someone loving and caring draw close to her in her time of need. She didn't see him coming. She was too consumed in her pain, her eyes blinded by all of her tears. That's when he arrived. That's when the pastor took her by the hand and personally led her to see her desire fulfilled.

I'm not quite sure how it happened, but tragedy soon struck. A hard life of poverty, malnutrition, and disease probably had its way with her. The young girl who had sat week after week in Sunday school, her smile beaming from cheek to cheek and her eyes glued on the teacher, suddenly passed away. When she passed, her little red purse caught the attention of a few people. She had carried it with her regularly. It wasn't anything fancy. You probably wouldn't give a quarter for it at a secondhand store. It wouldn't be on Etsy or Amazon. Purses like that one, torn and tattered, usually find their way into the garbage can. But not this time.

Hattie May had proudly carried it with her to church every week. When she passed, the family asked the church to assist with her funeral. The pastor, always wondering what was inside that little red purse, asked permission to peek into it. Inside he found a handful of coins and a little note. That note read something like, "This is to make the Sunday school room bigger so other boys and girls can hear about Jesus." I'm sure the spelling and grammar were horrific. But I guarantee the heart behind the words was spotless.

That young girl, who didn't have much to her name, had stopped to pick up spare coins every time she walked down the road to church, the park, or to pick something up for her family. Little spare coins, not worth much to someone like you and me. After all, we are too busy to stop and pick up those pennies. Most of us, when we order a cup of coffee or a hot dog and are handed back a few coins, drop them in the little container right by the cash register. What good can come from a few little coins?

But what was overlooked by so many was not overlooked by Hattie. She dared to slow down long enough to notice what was right in front of her. It didn't seem like much—it usually doesn't—but miracles are in disguise all around us. Yes, even in the valley of the shadow of death.

At her funeral, the pastor charged the deacon board and congregation to honor Hattie May's faith. People were inspired by this young girl who saved coin after coin, believing it could make a difference. Her plan was to give the money so more children could hear about Jesus. Word got out about the young girl's generous gift and childlike faith. People began to give their own money—thousands of dollars in a short amount of time. A piece of property came up for sale. Church leadership was made aware of the lucrative piece of real estate. The location was ideal, but there was no way they could afford it. Even with the thousands of dollars coming in from generous donors in honor of Hattie May, it just wouldn't be enough. But God had another plan.

The piece of property was sold to the church with a down payment of the exact amount of coins found in the deceased child's purse: 57 cents.

Next time you're in Philadelphia, visit Temple University, where some of our country's finest study in its classrooms to make a difference in various spheres of society. The university's performing arts center sits on the very spot that previously held Hattie's Baptist Temple. Make sure to notice Temple University Hospital, where many little children receive timely and excellent health care to prevent tragedies such as hers.

All of these amazing buildings and more are traced back to the initial faith and courage of a young child who dared to slow down long enough to notice. She dared to believe that her circumstances could very well be the path to a miracle for others. I can just imagine God making sure she walked down the right road, at just the right time, to pick up each coin. One by one. When we see the path God prepares for us, it can literally launch our dream in perpetuity.

Hope Is in Front of You

While Hattie May's path was paved with coins, David's path was paved with a father who overlooked him, family members who doubted him, a giant who taunted and bullied him, and a past

189

that tainted him. Saul threatened him and tried to murder him, bears and lions tried to maul him, and Hereth tried to discourage him. What a horrible path to take, right? But David said God leads us in multiple paths, and they are all righteous ones. *He leads us in paths of righteousness.* Why? For *the sake of his name.* Right now, at the very place you are at in life, *his goodness and mercy have followed you,* and he is ever-present. Your circumstance doesn't need to change before you taste his goodness. You may have a handful of coins or many heartbreaks in front of you. Either way, he stops and kneels down as you sit beside the road, alone.

For a moment, stop and reflect about where you truly are in life. Did you ever foresee a day when you would be where you are? Your family may be healthy and thriving, or maybe it's falling apart. You and your friends may have made a commitment to always be there for one another, or you may be walking all alone. Do you fight to go to sleep because of what you may see when you close your eyes? Do you dread one more conversation because you have run out of words?

If you have to manufacture energy just to get through something, God invites you to overcome. If you are okay with just coping in certain areas of your life, God invites you to his extravagant grace. What would your life look like if you could start over and rewrite it? What does the next chapter in your story look like? In Christ, a new chapter is possible. So is a new story.

Some are so far from hope that this idea seems ridiculous. Others have tried to embrace God's hope and just can't handle another disappointment. Scripture says if we wait on God we will never be put to shame (see Isa. 49:23). Am I asking you to reach out to God once more for his grace to empower you as you walk through your valley? Yes.

What other option worth choosing do you have, anyway?

Your life may be abundant and full of promise; indeed, for many of us it is at times. Some reading this book can't relate to the violation of trust we discussed or the deep pain some have walked through. I thank God for that. I also know many reading this right now truly feel boxed in emotionally, mentally, socially, financially, physically, or spiritually. There are areas where we desperately need hope to break in and grace to arise. For some, grace seems to have run out. For some, the tears stopped a long time ago. For all of us, God is reaching out to us wherever our path has led. It is his goodness that followed you into your valley, and you knew it not.

David slowed down long enough in the forest of Hereth to notice, just like Hattie May did, that his world was paved by the divine. As he reflected over his life in this moment of deep pain and turmoil, he would see all along that what he desperately needed had been given by God—time and time again. This is how we come to the place where we see God's grace in our valley right now. We dare to look for a time in our lives when his character and his Word have failed us. We will never find such a thing.

God Will Find You

We need to look at those early years in David's life one last time to see how God groomed David all along to become a captive to divine grace. He saw the table God prepared for him right in the presence of his enemies. It was there that his head was anointed with oil and his cup overflowed.

Ancient Hebrew kings had their heads anointed with oil. The oil itself did not make the person king; rather, it identified the one God had picked. David was anointed with oil, we read in 1 Samuel 16, when the prophet Samuel came to Jesse's house. God told the prophet to go there, for the next king of Israel would fall within his eyeshot. Samuel obeyed. And the prophet found himself in a unique situation. Jesse had numerous sons and, as Samuel fixed his gaze on each of them, he thought, *Surely he is the one.* After all, God always chooses the strongest and most prolific leaders, right?

Of course not. Samuel was tricked by what he saw as he fell prey to looking at their outward appearance. But God always looks at the heart.

I can just imagine Samuel asking David's father, Jesse, "Is this all of the sons you have? Listen, God literally told me to come here. I know for a fact the next king of Israel is supposed to be chosen right here, today, and I am not going anywhere until it happens. So, what's up, Jesse?"

The Scripture reveals that Jesse did have another son, David. David's leadership ability, his reputation, and his background so disqualified him that even his own father did not think to invite him home when the prophet showed up. But God sees what we don't see. It still amazes me that God sent the prophet Samuel to Jesse's house knowing full well David was not there. David was out in the pasture, tending the sheep, being faithful when no one was looking. Let me rephrase that: faithful when no *person* was looking. God saw David.

Why didn't God send Samuel to the field where David was? That would have saved everyone some embarrassment. But sometimes God sends the prophet to the house knowing full well the next king is not in the house. What do you do, Samuel, when you know God promised you something, and your circumstance does not line up? Do you doubt? Do you leave? Unfortunately, many of us would, but Samuel trusted God even when his circumstance gave him a reason not to. Samuel waited for the promise to come, for he dared to rely on what he knew to be true about God regardless of any cognitive reason to give in to unbelief. And David did come.

David's head was anointed with oil. He was chosen, not by the popular vote but by God, to rule as king. But David didn't move immediately into the castle where he would be surrounded by bodyguards. No, he was dispatched to go back to the field as a shepherd boy. He went away and stepped up to take on the giant. He went away and was ridiculed by a leader he served honorably. He went away and was overlooked time and time again. If you had asked anyone there at the time who the king of Israel was, their answer would be Saul. If you had asked God who the king of Israel was, his answer would be David.

Sometimes a reality in heaven initially looks different from the reality on the earth. But those who dare to be vulnerable can embrace what Scripture alludes to in Matthew 6:10: that one day, long before we enter heaven, heaven will once again invade the earth and infuse our situation. The goal is for heaven's promise to become real in our day.

While in the Hereth forest, David recounted that time he was anointed with oil by Samuel. It is here, in circumstances that starkly contrast what any newly appointed king would expect, that he looked back over his life and came face-to-face with the assurance that God had never failed him before. I'm sure he asked himself, *Why would God change and start failing me now?*

David, you teach us all how accessible grace is in our valley.

He sang and recited—not in the green pasture but in the valley of the shadow of death—of his experience in becoming king. Kings are chosen in the valley. That's where their head, and our head, are anointed with oil. You may not realize it, but your heartbreak and disappointment may very well be an invitation by heaven to step into your royal position. At the barren place where he was a lowly shepherd, David was crowned. During his dark night of the soul, David imagined that same experience, and the landscape was a valley.

Something else happened in the valley when David imagined the aroma of oil running down his head. His cup was not filled halfway nor to the top but overflowed. David, like many other Middle Eastern shepherds, would've been familiar with a certain custom, and there are some parts of the world today where this custom is still observed. A male-dominated society and a nomadic lifestyle have led families to experience something time and time again.

When God Asks Us to Stay

Wandering around the desert surrounded by sheep doesn't serve one well hygienically. As the sun would set and a shepherd readied his family to set up camp, perhaps off in the distance he would see a campfire. Approaching someone else's camp would open up a realm of hospitality many Westerners do not understand. As he would venture toward that other family's dwelling, the male leader of that family or clan would step outside and greet him. There they would be, two men standing face-to-face in a dry and barren place. One of the men is prepared for the night to come and the other hopes to receive some assistance. Without saying a word, the first shepherd takes a horn or flask of oil and hands it to the shepherd seeking assistance.

I've been told this oil has two primary purposes. One, the oil is aromatic and provided relief from the stench of body odor. After all, the shepherd has probably wandered around the desert for quite some time and the benefits of modern society, like deodorant and a shower, are not accessible at that time. The oil would be poured on the head of the shepherd, and then he would turn around and do the same to his family. The scent of flowers and spice would fill the air and for a moment the travelers would feel and smell clean again. The oil, however, also had a second purpose. It was medicinal, rumored to cure head lice and sanitize. The last thing anyone would want would be to invite a wandering family into your tent to enjoy a meal, and then they leave some disease behind.

Once their heads were anointed with oil, the family would be invited to sit in the tent or beside it to enjoy a meal consisting of flatbread, raisin cakes, curds, honey, and perhaps a few other luxuries from time to time such as meat. Both families would enjoy the food and conversation. At the end of the meal, without saying a word, the male leader of the inviting family would go up to the male leader of the guest family. Holding out a wineskin, the host would begin to pour into his guest's cup. If the cup was filled halfway, it was the host's way of saying, "The conversation has been good, but you must be on your way soon." But if the cup was filled up to the top, well, that's another story.

Filling the cup all the way to the top is a way of saying, "You are our guests of honor, we enjoy your company very much, and we want to talk more." The families would stay up into the late evening, where music and laughter could fill the night air. The shepherds would sit around the fire and perhaps use the carvings in their rod and staff to remember all the great stories of old. These "journals" were read as a celebration to God for his mercy and intervention in their lives. Their rod and staff, around that campfire, comforted them. In the morning, after the long night of jubilation, the families would enjoy one more meal together before they separated and continued to walk their respective paths, wherever they may lead. If those Hebrew shepherds are like us—and they are—then we know some would walk the path to a green pasture and others quite possibly to the valley of the shadow of death. But it's only a shadow.

David envisioned a God in his valley who reached out to him as the table was being prepared. David's head was anointed with oil and his cup was filled neither halfway nor to the top—it overflowed. God is incapable of moderately loving us. His love is extravagant. His presence is breathtaking. God keeps pouring and pouring. I can picture you saying, "God, you can stop pouring now. It's getting full—it's—God! Wait! Now it's falling all over the place. It's dripping on the tablecloth. This amazing meal, this dinner you prepared and personally invited me to—you're ruining your table setting just because you won't stop pouring and pouring and pouring."

Does God not know what he is doing? Hardly.

God wants to pour stability into your finances. I'm not suggesting that being a millionaire is everyone's destiny. I do know, however, that God doesn't want you to be anxious or stressed about how your needs will be met. God can pour wholeness into your heart. You will once again know how to be vulnerable and laugh, unafraid your world will come crashing down tomorrow.

You can enjoy this day and all its pleasures, and expect an even better day to come.

When God keeps pouring and pouring, you dare to dream again and confidently rest in who you are in Christ. Your spiritual cup overflows as Scripture comes alive to you, and your daily life is impacted for the better because you connect divine promises with day-to-day living. When truth is needed, the enemy of confusion will leave. When a life-changing decision is needed and you're terrified of making the wrong call, wisdom flows over the sides of your cup as God guides you in the correct path. You may stand alone at times, but God's presence overflows and reveals you are never alone. You may grieve deeply at what your life could have been, or wish you could go back, but God's grace continuously pours out and spills over all areas of your life, making even the deadest of places in your valley change color.

Blessing Pursues You

What you consider waste, God considers blessing. He keeps pouring and pouring. It is God's way of inviting you closer. He wants to sit around with you, just like those Hebrew shepherds, and take the rod and staff and comfort you. He wants you to remember, with him, all of the times when you stood in a valley and watched it bloom. The realm of intimacy with God David speaks of does not occur in the green pasture but in the valley. Now we understand how David could emphatically declare toward the end of his song, *Surely goodness and mercy will follow me all the days of my life, and I will dwell in the house of the LORD forever.* The Hebrew for "follow me" can literally mean "pursue or chase me." It's much more than God's goodness going wherever you go. The language used depicts a God who will make sure his goodness will eventually catch up to you, and you will experience a collision with him.

God's goodness and mercy relentlessly pursue you at a pace much faster than anything else.

The new king of Israel isn't interested in living in the king's castle. He isn't fixated on a plush palace surrounded by loyal soldiers. He isn't bitter at King Saul for the pain and heartache. He isn't jaded or cynical with God for the situation he found himself in—a situation, by the way, God could have easily prevented. Although while in Hereth anywhere safe would look attractive, David locks his eyes on dwelling in God's house. He makes it abundantly clear, first and foremost to himself, that he will *dwell in the house of the LORD forever*. David's primal craving is for God alone (as is the case with us all, regardless of our consciousness of it).

There is a place we can come to in life where what we see is not all there is. To deny heartache and pretend all is well is to be inhuman. David did not deny his reality. He acknowledged the enemy at hand. He recognized the steep embankment of the valley he wandered into. His heart was also open to embrace the table prepared for him by God in a circumstance highly unusual and hard to comprehend.

For those who stand in the barren place void of rain, wondering if life can come forth, be encouraged. Like he did with Hattie May, God can take what little you see in your current situation and perform a miracle that will long outlast anything you can imagine.

For those who still see so many things written on your chalkboard and cannot even make out the good written beside the bad, be at peace. God can and will send the rain, and your desert will bloom once again. God sees you in your quiet desperation and, like the young boy, declares over you, "But I still love you." When your circumstance does not line up with the God you know in your heart of hearts is real, just know: the green pasture and the valley of the shadow of death are actually the same place. But you knew that all along. You just needed someone who is not in your particular valley to say so.

When I am in my valley, do me a favor and remind me of the same.

Afterword

When we ask the infamous "why" questions of God, often we end up thinking, *Well, God just has a plan.* God does indeed know the outcome of our situations and weaves purpose in and out of it (Jer. 29:11). This notion, though, can be a psychological crutch to appease our longing for answers. What we need is faith, and faith is not crossing our fingers and making a wish. Faith is a substance (Heb. 11:1), something tangible we can hold in our hands. In my experience, the substance of our faith is often comprised of pieces of wisdom we gain when we walk from the green pasture into the valley and sit at God's table. David unwrapped quite a few of these for us in Psalm 23.

In closing, I want to empower you with some core concepts I've personally learned from Psalm 23 for you to read frequently, memorize, or pray about whenever you walk into the valley.

Identity is shaped (*The LORD is my shepherd*). Who God is and who you are come front and center. David said God was his Shepherd. David knew he was one of God's sheep.

Reality is assessed (*I shall not want*). David no longer wanted what he very well could have on a good day. In Hereth, what you need takes precedent over what you want.

Purpose is realized (*He makes me lie down in green pastures*). David saw God's heart motivation was to create a place for David to lie down.

God's perspective is gained (*He leads me beside still waters*). Yes, the waters are always still.

Restoration continues (*He restores my soul*). Attributing reason and casting blame are not as important as seeing your reflection in God's eyes.

Meaning is derived (*He leads me in paths of righteousness for his name's sake*). One greater than you bows low just to walk at your side, for it is ultimately God's story.

Emotional intelligence is strengthened (*Even though I walk through the valley of the shadow of death, I will fear no evil*). We embrace how we feel but refuse to get stuck there. God can process with us as his kingdom becomes our reality.

Isolation is eliminated (*For you are with me*). Quiet desperation, shame, or hopelessness do not need to rob you any longer. You are not alone.

Truth is revealed (*Your rod and your staff, they comfort me*). Our self-talk can be aligned with God's Word and our responses can sync with the Holy Spirit's prompting.

Understanding evolves (*You prepare a table before me in the presence of my enemies*). What you thought was God's judgment against you or a spiritual attack is actually an invitation to feast in God's presence. There is a special place at his table just for you. And no one else can take that place.

Intimacy is experienced (*You anoint my head with oil and my cup overflows*). Incapable of moderately loving us, God faithfully comes to us in our difficult seasons. In his presence, we discover our royal position, and our longings are satisfied in him. The table of blessing is not relegated to healing, provision, the miraculous, or deliverance. Ultimately, God's presence is our table.

Assurance is established (*Surely goodness and mercy will follow me all the days of my life*). Circumstances no longer define our hopes—they catalyze them. God is never taken by surprise. When we look into his face in prayer and adoration, we do not see a God who is aloof or haphazardly engaged. God loves us dearly, and we do not need to pursue goodness and mercy, for they will pursue us.

Hope is tangible (*I will dwell in the house of the Lord forever*). Forever doesn't begin when you step from this life to the next. Forever has no beginning, for God has no beginning. You are temporarily passing through this life; however, you are in the midst of forever right now, for the Ancient One dwells within you by his Spirit. You and I do not wait until after we die to experience his presence. Heaven is a real place, and in Christ we will be there with him forever. I am grateful for this. Dwelling in God's house has as much to do with your life here and now as it does eternity.

Let heaven come and surround you in the place you are.

Notes

Chapter 1 Learning to See

1. Del Tarr, "Making Truth Memorable," *Christianity Today*, accessed May 1, 2018, https://www.christianitytoday.com/pastors/1983/spring/8312066.html.

Chapter 2 Does God Recognize You?

1. Catherine Wynne, "The Teenager Who Saved a Man with an SS Tattoo," *BBC News*, October 29, 2013, http://www.bbc.com/news/magazine-24653643.

2. "1988 Armenian Earthquake," *Wikipedia*, accessed May 1, 2018, https://en.wikipedia.org/wiki/1988_Armenian_earthquake; "Armenia Earthquake December 1988," *International Rescue Corps*, accessed May 1, 2018, http://www.intrescue.info/hub/index.php/missions/armenia-earthquake-december-1988/.

3. Max Lucado, *When Christ Comes* (Nashville: Thomas Nelson, 1999), 21–22.

4. Lucado, *When Christ Comes*, 22.

Chapter 3 What We See in the Valley

1. T. S. Eliot, "Choruses from 'The Rock,'" *The Complete Poems and Plays: 1909–1950* (Orlando: Harcourt Brace, 1971), 96.

2. Tony Long, "July 2, 1982: Up, Up and Away with 42 Balloons," *Wired*, July 2, 2009, https://www.wired.com/2009/07/dayintech-0702/.

3. Myrna Oliver, "Larry Walters; Soared to Fame on Lawn Chair," *LA Times*, November 24, 1993, http://articles.latimes.com/1993-11-24/news /mn-60236_1_larry-walters.

4. Oliver, "Larry Walters; Soared to Fame on Lawn Chair."

Chapter 5 Beside Still Waters

1. Scott Stump, "'God's Angels': Human Chain of Almost 80 Strangers Save a Drowning Family," *Today*, July 12, 2017, https://www.today.com /news/beachgoers-form-human-chain-save-family-rip-current-t113744.

2. Harold Kushner, *The Lord Is My Shepherd* (New York: Random House, 2003).

Chapter 6 Running in the Night

1. James Rutz, *Mega Shift* (Colorado Springs: Empowerment Press, 2005).

Chapter 7 Pieces and Lids

1. Max Lucado, *No Wonder They Call Him the Savior* (Nashville: Thomas Nelson, 1986) 158–59.

2. Aida Manduley, "The Real Origin of the African Birth Song: Surprise, It's Racist," *Aida Manduley, MSW*, March 10, 2015, http://aidaman duley.com/2015/03/10/the-real-origin-of-the-african-birth-song/.

Chapter 8 Whose Shadow Is It, Anyway?

1. "Fire Ants Help a Near Dead Skydiver Survive a 14,500 Foot Fall from the Sky," Skydiving.com, February 26, 2017, https://www.skydiving.co m/news/2017/skydiving/accidents/female-skydiving-enthusiast-survives plummeting-14500-feet-onto-fire-ant-mound/.

2. Joseph Berger, "Man in the News; Witness to Evil: Eliezer Weisel," *New York Times*, October 15, 1986, https://www.nytimes.com/1986/10/15 /world/man-in-the-news-witness-to-evil-eliezer-weisel.html.

3. Max Ehrmann, "Desiderata," accessed May 2, 2018, http://mwkworks .com/desiderata.html.

Chapter 9 Comforted by Engraved Stories

1. "A Victim Treats His Mugger Right," *NPR*, March 28, 2008, https:// www.npr.org/2008/03/28/89164759/a-victim-treats-his-mugger-right.

2. Caroline Leaf, *Who Switched Off My Brain?* (Nashville: Thomas Nelson, 2009), 21–23.

3. Peter Dizikes, "When the Butterfly Effect Took Flight," *MIT Technology Review*, February 22, 2011, https://www.technologyreview.com/s/422809/when-the-butterfly-effect-took-flight/.

4. Camilla Townsend, "Burying the White Gods: New Perspectives on the Conquest of Mexico," *The American Historical Review*, vol. 108 no. 3, (June 1, 2003): 659–87, https://doi.org/10.1086/ahr/108.3.659; Maurice Cotterell, "Historical Notes: A Feathered Snake and a Man with a Beard," *Independent*, January 15, 1999, https://www.independent.co.uk/arts-entertainment/historical-notes-a-feathered-snake-and-a-man-with-a-beard-1047064.html; Robert Wauchope, ed., *Handbook of Middle American Indians*, vol. 13 part 2 (Austin: University of Texas Press, 1973).

Chapter 10 The Table Your Enemy Can't Feast At

1. "About the Holocaust: Rescue," *Yad Vashem*, accessed May 2, 2018, http://www.yadvashem.org/holocaust/about/rescue.html.

2. "'Women of Valor': Stories of Women Who Rescued Jews During the Holocaust," *Yad Vashem*, accessed May 2, 2018, http://www.yadvashem.org/yv/en/exhibitions/righteous-women/sendler.asp; "Life in a Jar: The Irena Sendler Project," accessed May 2, 2018, http://www.irenasendler.org/.

Chapter 11 A Realm of Intimacy

1. "The History of Fifty-Seven Cents," Temple University, accessed May 2, 2018, https://library.temple.edu/collections/scrc/hattie; Ed Delph, "57 Cents That Made History," *The Glendale Star*, August 24, 2011, http://www.glendalestar.com/opinion/columns/article_3094091a-cd9f-11e0-af0e-001cc4c002e0.html.

Heath Adamson's life was changed dramatically when, at the age of seventeen, he was saved out of a life steeped in drug abuse and the occult. Now a popular and powerful speaker at conferences, seminars, universities, and churches, Adamson seeks to bring audiences from simply knowing information about God to actually experiencing God in life-changing ways. God's grace has led him to serve in multiple leadership roles with global influence. Currently, he serves at Convoy of Hope (www.convoyofhope.org), a global nonprofit focused on God's compassion and justice, where loving the poor and needy is a privilege. He is also the global chairman for the Next Gen Commission for the World Assemblies of God Fellowship, a community of over 360,000 churches. He is currently a PhD candidate in Religious Studies at the University of London. He and his wife, Ali, are inheriting God's dream together with their two daughters, Leighton and Dallon. As a family, they know God always has more for them and for you.

"SELDOM RESIST THE IMPULSE TO **DO SOMETHING KIND.**"

Hal Donaldson

CONVOY OF HOPE®

WWW.CONVOYOFHOPE.ORG

As a faith-based, nonprofit organization, Convoy of Hope has helped more than eighty million people throughout the world by sharing food, water, emergency supplies, agricultural know-how, and opportunities that empower people to live independent lives, free from poverty, disease, and hunger.